David Ranney's *Tennis: Play the Mental Game* provides clear, easy to follow "mini lessons" and tips that will benefit players of any level. Since reading "The Inner game of Tennis" by Tim Gallwey so many years ago, I have not seen another book that addresses such an essential aspect of tennis so well. Watch your game get better and better as you experience what playing the mental game is all about.

Billie Jean King, winner of six Wimbledon singles championships and four US Open Championships.

Although brief in length, David Ranney's *Tennis: Play the Mental Game* is long on useful information. Written from the perspective of a player, this is the kind of advice that makes sense from the first reading. You don't need a Ph D to understand how to benefit immediately from this work. If you have ever played below your level, had problems with your temper or felt the frustration in playing this wonderful game of tennis David's book is definitely the remedy!

Ron Waite, USPTR
Author of the column, Turbo Tennis.
www.tennisserver.com

I love improvement and your ideas have been terrific to that end. I have another disciple in "the fold" as I let him read your book. He has been practicing both "core" foundations; breathing and watching. He has improved also. He is a 50 yr. old 4.5 player. His wife noticed him mumbling his mantra while studying the "core" and promptly took it away from him and now she is in "the fold" as well. We may have started a groundswell. I even have another friend studying it and his initial reaction was "I'm too old to learn new tricks!" Au contraire!

I am where I can see the ball actually slow after it lands allowing my feeble mind time to relax and execute the shot as opposed to reacting to the initial rate of pace during its' flight. That is interesting to watch. The BIGGEST benefit of all is just keeping all the other SPAM debris or conscious thought from interfering with actual play. It is such a relaxing way to play; mindless.

George Kraft, Seattle, WA

David's principles will make you a believer in the paradox that by "letting go" you achieve more. Wait until you experience a mind and body that has "let go", is calm, and relaxed; it feels unbelievably fun! You will achieve greater focus, concentration and results on the tennis court.

Carla Lyons, Bellingham, WA

David's teaching and his book Tennis: Play The Mental Game is by far the single best way for you to improve your game and your enjoyment of the game. His simple yet effective tools for focusing the mind changed my game entirely. David taught me how to focus my mind upon the ball, about relaxation, and about breathing instead of the details of stroke. Now there is not that constant war in my head about how to hit each and every ball (and then how I hit it incorrectly). Instead, I my mind lets my body hit the strokes I know I have and allows me to have the confidence to play my game.

By changing my focus away from the details of each shot and towards the playing of the game, I simply have more fun with tennis. With David's help, I've had more fun playing tennis in the last three years that I did in the previous 30.

Doug Robertson, owner, Bellingham Tennis Club. Doug's been playing since age 9 and is now on the other side of 40.

Thanks Dave!!!! I've put what you taught me into practice and it's made an incredible difference for me. I think it's the biggest revelation I've ever experienced in my 20 some odd years of trying to get better at this game.

Alisa Hashimoto, Seattle, WA

TENNIS:
Play the Mental Game

By David Ranney

Published by

Night Lotus Books

PO Box 701

Cardiff by the Sea, CA 92007

www.nightlotusbooks.com

Printed in the U.S.A. by Print & Copy Factory, Bellingham, Washington
www.printcopyfactory.com

ISBN 0-9785568-2-8
ISBN 13 978-0-9785568-2-2
Library of Congress number: 2006926589

Publisher's Cataloging-in-Publication data

Ranney, David Edward.

Tennis : play the mental game and be "in the zone" every time you play /
David Ranney.

p. cm.

Includes index.

ISBN 0-9785568-2-8
ISBN 13 978-0-9785568-2-2

1. Tennis--Psychological aspects. I. Title.

GV1002.9.P75 R35 2006

796.342-dc22   LC# 2006926589

Acknowledgments

I want to acknowledge many people who have helped me with this book. First, I would like to thank all my students who have given me the opportunity to test my lessons. I always knew these ideas worked on me, but without my students using these principles, I would not have known whether they would work on anyone else. Once I started this book, still others gave me editing, organizational, and other kinds of help. These people are (in no particular order) Sharon Janis, who not only designed the front and back cover but gave me so much advice on publishing that I could not have done this book without her, my daughter, Jolie, who helped me with editing, Ken Stuart, Dick Leach, John Webb, Larry Horowitz, Terry Harmer, Myra Harmer, who help with the formatting, Doug Nyland, and Tana Silva (editor). A special thanks to Dr. Dave Dobson, my "Other Than Conscious" expert and friend, for helping me make the language as effective as possible.

Contents

Foreword

If you are reading this, two things are certain: You are likely serious about your tennis, and you believe there is something out there that is going to make you a better tennis player. This book is it!

During my tennis teaching days, I was often asked; "Ken, can you teach me a forehand, backhand, overhead smash, footwork, etc." I always answered in the affirmative and followed it with, "Oh yeah, I can also teach you how to play tennis because they (your strokes) are not much related to playing the game."

Rarely, if ever, do you have the opportunity to read something that has been written first hand. This book will make you a better tennis player because the information in it is tried, tested and true. And it comes from a great tennis player in his own right; David Ranney. Dave's experience speaks for itself, and his advice in this book is solid. Here are some questions you can ask yourself to determine the value of the content in this book.

1. Who has a better forehand, Roger Federer or Andre Agassi?

2. Who has a better backhand, Lindsay Davenport or Serena Williams?

3. Who was a better player, Pete Sampras or Rod Laver?

The answer to each of these questions is that it is essentially indistinguishable. The logical conclusion is then that if "strokes" don't make the difference among all these greats then what does? EXACTLY!

It is the mental part of the game that each of these people is commonly great at. You too can become a much, much better player without changing your strokes. The great coach Robert Van't Hof once said; "If you do the right thing at the right time in tennis you are likely going to win." The catch is how do you get there? This book will give you a path to follow. Use it and you'll be miles ahead of people you are equal with now.

You need only to look back at how many countless hours you have put into the development of your strokes. Now you have to spend the same dedication on the mental part of your game. Dave Ranney will guide you through the steps you need to practice to become a much better tennis player.

Ken Stuart, Owner of Palisades Tennis Club,
Newport Beach and former world class player

Chapter 1 - Introduction to the Mental Game

About This Book

Congratulations on choosing this book. The simple fact that you have even looked at a book on the mental game means that what you are doing now isn't working so well and you are searching for a better way.

When I start working with new students, I always ask them what percentage of the game of tennis they think is mental. They usually answer somewhere between 75 and 95 percent. I then ask them what percentage of the time they actually practice their mental game. Most of them will say "very little" or "not at all." My next question is, if they were going to practice the mental game, how would they do it? Again, most of the time the answer is either some very vague idea or "I don't know." After reading this book, you will not only know what the mental game is, but you will know how to play it and it will never be a mystery again.

This book will spell out very precisely what playing the mental game looks like and how you will know if you are doing it justice. It is the result of over 25 years of studying, practicing, and teaching the mental game.

After you read this book and put these principles into play, you will be entering a whole different world of tennis, one that will speed up your learning and help you to enjoy the game more. Best of all, you will find yourself playing better. However, there is a catch. You still have to read this book and not only believe in the mental game -- you have to practice it and truly play it.

In this book, I don't get into the whole philosophy behind the mental game, as I feel you can get this much better from reading Timothy Gallwey's *The Inner Game of Tennis*. In fact, Gallwey's book is really required reading, as it will give you the background to what I am trying to teach you. In my opinion, the other present-day books on the philosophy of the mental game pretty much say what Tim Gallwey was saying over 30 years ago, only not as eloquently. My book is a natural extension to Gallwey's book as it offers hands-on and practical strategies rather than a general philosophical approach.

I have divided this book into four parts: Mental Concepts, Strategy, Strokes and How to Practice (Drills). The mental part will focus on how to find the mental state you need to be in to play "in the zone." The strategy part will give you some new ideas on how to play your opponent and where to hit the ball. The stroke part will help you develop relaxed and consistent strokes as well as teach you how to practice these strokes. In the How to Practice section, I have 14 terrific drills for you to do. However, the mental part always comes first, because mastering the mental part of the game so you can play in the zone remains the ultimate goal.

About David Ranney

I started playing tournaments when I was 10 years old. I became a nationally ranked player (*see my complete resume on my Web site, www.maxtennis.com/my_resume.htm*) as a junior, played on the USC tennis team with Stan Smith and Bob Lutz (we were National Champions during the three years I lettered Varsity), played on the Junior Davis Cup team, and represented the U.S. at Junior Wimbledon when I was 17 years old.

After college, I began teaching tennis the traditional way until my conversion to teaching the Inner Game when I was in my 30s.

In the 25 plus years since then, I have been studying the mental game so that I could achieve the state of mind that will maximize my tennis game. I wanted to know how to play "out of my mind" every time I played. I now believe I have found out how to do this. It is easy to talk about, but it takes practice to get there. As I was trying to discover this mental technique for myself, I had varying degrees of success at first, but as time passed and after a lot of experimenting, I have come up with a very easy way to play the mental game.

I knew that these ideas worked for me, but I didn't know if they would work for anybody else. Over the years I have worked with enough beginners, average players and good tournament players to know that it works and that anyone can do it.

What I Know About You

As a psychic, I have looked into my crystal ball and I will tell all. You love the game of tennis, but you feel that you are just not playing the best you can. At times (maybe most of the time), you are not enjoying yourself because you are getting more and more frustrated and you just don't know why you are missing so many balls. You are trying so hard to stroke the ball correctly, trying so hard to play well, and trying so hard to win, and you just can't seem to make it happen. You want more from tennis, and so you are searching for a different or better way of playing.

So, how did I do? Do you still think I am psychic? That will be $10, please.

Why Play The Mental Game?

By playing the mental game you will be developing the relationship between your "conscious mind," your "other than conscious mind," and your body. It is your other than conscious mind that directs the body, which then hits the ball and achieves the ideal tennis play. The strength, direction, and quality of your outer tennis strokes are determined by this inner relationship. When you pursue and find this ideal mental state, you will be playing in the zone.

As a natural by-product, you will find that your enjoyment of your tennis game will be enhanced. This is because you will be calmer and more relaxed, and of course, you will be playing better.

The Ultimate Goal

The ultimate goal is for you to find out how to play your very best every time by finding the state of mind you have to be in to play in the zone. I cannot describe to you what this state of mind feels like, but I can guide you so that you can begin to discover for yourself how to get there. Notice that I did not say that the ultimate goal is to win (see Lesson #1).

The path to this state of mind can be found in the Mental Game Core Principles, which you'll find at the end of this chapter. As you begin to master these Core Principles, you will be on the road to discovering how to play in the zone every time you play. Mastering these Core Principles may be a lifelong process. You will be discovering things about yourself and your game for the rest of your life. And who knows, maybe you will find some of these principles useful in other areas of your life as well.

How to Make These Lessons Work for You

To maximize the benefits of this book, first familiarize yourself with the Mental Game Core Principles. These principles will give you the foundation for every tip, idea, and instruction in this book. I suggest that you keep a copy of my book with you so that you can read these principles every time before you play. *Using these core principles are an absolute must for tournament play.*

The *Mini Lessons* in this book are listed in order of importance. Therefore, I suggest that you start from the

17

beginning. Every lesson is important in your development, but if you need help with a particular aspect of your game, you may want to skip ahead to those lessons that are applicable.

You'll find that some solutions to the problem are repeated in different lessons. This is because the same "fix" is often good for more than one issue. As you read through the lessons, you will discover that many of the same solutions work for a variety of situations when you get off track mentally.

I have left a lot of white space between paragraphs, between chapters, and between lessons for you to make notes or comments on what is going on as you work with these ideas. Therefore, this book can and should be used as a workbook, so take it with you when you play.

Questions and comments on the mental game are welcome. E-mail me at david@maxtennis.com.

The Best Lesson I Ever Received

The best lesson I ever received wasn't really just one lesson, but a whole new way of playing. I used to yell and scream on the tennis court because I would get so frustrated. I thought that if I could only stroke the ball perfectly I would never miss. But of course, I couldn't do that every time, and boy did I try hard. My attitude was horrible. I hated myself for getting so angry and frustrated, but I couldn't stop. I had no idea why I played badly at times, why I never beat players who were just a little better than I was, and I didn't have a clue as to how to turn my game around when I wasn't playing well. I don't think anyone tried harder than I did.

Then one day (I was in my 30s), I was reading the *LA Magazine* about an instructor who was teaching the *Inner Game of Tennis*. His name was Tim Gallwey. I knew I had to have a lesson from this man, and I was determined to go to the ends of the earth to find him. As it turned out, he was right there in my hometown of Los Angeles.

To make a long story longer, I took two lessons from Tim, and he completely changed my life as a player. After the first lesson from him, I never got angry or yelled again – an amazing accomplishment since I had already spent most of my tennis life getting upset with my play. My doubles partner at the time, Keith Nielson, whom I played once a week said that it wasn't as much fun to play me anymore because he couldn't get me angry.

All of a sudden my tennis game was more consistent, and overnight my endurance increased. I wasn't so tense all the time, and this shift allowed me to keep my energy focused on mastering the mental game. For the first time, I was beating people I could never beat before. I was winning close matches and hitting balls that I never had been able to hit before. To sum it all up, I felt like the world was taken off my back when I was on the court.

After I took the two lessons from Tim Gallwey, he not only completely changed my own tennis game but also my whole way of teaching. I asked Tim to come to the Jack Kramer Tennis Club, where I was an assistant teaching pro under Robert Lansdorp, so he could give clinics to all of my students. There I watched Tim in action. As a result, I adapted his ideas and modified them slightly to fit my own way of teaching.

I will be forever grateful to Tim Gallwey for showing me how to make this change. His book has been my "Tennis Bible" and is truly one of the best books ever written on the mental aspects of the game. You can get his book by going to his Web site, (www.theinnergame.com) or in most bookstores.

What Are the Core Principles of the Mental Game?

There are four primary parts to the Core Principles of the mental game: Consciousness, Focus, Breathing, and Judgment.

The Principles of Consciousness

We all have a "conscious mind" and an "other than conscious mind". The mental game encourages you to keep your conscious mind calm, clear, and out of the way while letting your other than conscious mind emerge. You can "program" your other than conscious mind with visualization and/or talking to yourself (see Dave Dobson's Beach CD at the end of this book).

The Principles of Focus

Focus lets you continually notice or pay attention to some aspect of your play. You use focus to put your attention on some part of your game that you want your other than conscious mind to respond to.

The Principles of Breathing

Breathing supplies the rhythm of relaxation. Proper breathing helps keep your upper body from getting tense, thereby allowing your other than conscious mind to use your body to its greatest potential.

The Principles of Playing Without Judgment

When you judge your shots, your strokes, how well you are playing, or anything else, it is unproductive and can even cause you to play worse. The natural response to your judgments is to try harder. This leads to using your conscious mind to start controlling your body, thereby becoming more tense. Although trying harder may seem to work in the short term, you will find that when the match gets tight or when it comes time to win, your game may break down.

In the following pages you will find the details of the Core Principles that should be anchored into your other than conscious mind. By activating these principles before you play and as needed during your playing, your conscious mind, your other than conscious mind, and your body will be in the best possible place to play at the top of your game.

The Mental Game Core Principles

Remember that the idea here is to truly get your conscious mind out of the way and turn over your play to your "other than conscious mind." The other than conscious mind's role is also to help you focus on the ball and your breathing. By programming yourself with these principles, you will be able to quickly and easily get into this state of mind. It just takes practice and discipline.

For those of you who want to go the extra mile in the fast lane, you will want to order the "Beach" audio CD (see details at the end of this book). This is a very sophisticated but very simple anchoring technique that will speed up your ability to let go and help you incorporate these Core Principles into your game.

The following statements make up the Core Principles: (Go to www.maxtennis.com/core_principles.htm if you want to print a copy of these Principles.)

- *Soon I will be able to pay attention and follow the ball all the way to my racket so that I can see the ball spinning. This is Core.*

- *As I learn to pay this kind of attention, I will soon be able to follow the ball and see it spinning from my racket all the way to my opponent's racket. This is Core.*

- *As I become more competent in paying attention to the ball, my breathing will become more natural, and I will learn to be exhaling with a sigh before making contact with the ball and exhaling through and long after contact with the ball. This is Core.*

- *I move for the ball and hit the ball "knowing" (see Lesson #13) where I want it to go without effort and without judgment. Without judgment means truly letting the ball go where it goes, truly accepting how well I am seeing the ball, truly accepting how well I am breathing, and truly accepting anything else that is happening while I am playing. This is Core.*

- *I observe my breathing and I watch the ball even in between points. This is Core.*

- *After missing a ball, if I feel it's necessary, I immediately visualize or talk to myself about hitting the ball into the court to the spot I would have liked it to go, using a perfect stroke, consciously seeing the ball perfectly, and consciously exhaling before and after contact with the ball. This is Core.*

- *My conscious mind stays calm and clear and I let my other than conscious mind direct my body to move to where I see the ball coming. This is Core.*

- *Between points, I sometimes inhale deeply and exhale slowly with a sigh to relax myself and clear my mind. This is Core.*

- *My strokes are smooth and relaxed through the entire stroke and my grip is very relaxed, especially at the point of contact. This is Core.*

- *My other than conscious mind is hitting the ball to where it "knows" to hit it while I am consciously seeing the ball and consciously exhaling before and after my hit. This is Core.*

- *When changing sides (always in tournaments) I sit down, clear my mind, relax my body and, if necessary, reprogram my other than conscious mind to do any of the above. This is Core.*

- *My other than conscious mind communicates to me any strategy changes to be made. If I am behind in the score, I will use the "wondering technique" given in Lesson #27 to determine what I need to do differently This is Core.*

- *In doing all of the above I am letting my other than conscious mind figure out how to make it happen, rather than trying to force myself to do anything by using my conscious mind. This is Core.*

Chapter 2 - Mental Concepts

Lesson #1 - About Winning: A Point to Ponder

I can tell you who has won every match that has ever been played, and I can tell you who will win every match that will be played in the future.

How can I make this statement?

Answer: The player who plays better on that given day will be the winner. So, if you play better than your opponent today, you will win.

The point of this is that winning will take care of itself, and if you strive and learn to play at the top of your game and that "top" makes you play better than your opponent, you will automatically win. And if you play twice as well as you ever had but still lose the game, most likely you will be a happy camper. I'm sorry, I meant to say a happy tennis player.

If you don't like how well you played (even though you played at the top of your game), then you need to figure out how you can play better in the future. This means that you will need to practice more of both the physical and the mental game. So, how do you play at the top of your game? See "The Mental Game Core Principles" in Chapter 1. And by spending more and more time using the concepts presented here and in *The Inner Game of Tennis,* you will find that your body will learn faster and more easily.

.sson #2 - On Seeing the Ball

If you were to ask me to pick the single most important thing to do when playing, I would say that you need to focus on seeing the ball. And you need to really, really see the ball properly. Unfortunately, most people don't see the ball the way it needs to be seen, even after being shown how to do it and told how important it is.

"See the ball." "Watch the ball." "Look at the ball." Yes, I know you have heard this so many times. But do you really consciously see the ball all the way to and from your racket? It is not as easy as it sounds. And as you get into really seeing the ball, it becomes easy to think that you are seeing the ball well when you really aren't.

When I talk about how important it is to really see the ball clearly, some of my students try so hard to focus on the ball that they tense up too much. Remember that you don't need to try hard to read the words on this page, and likewise you don't need to try hard to see things if you were to look up from this book and look around the room. The same principle applies to seeing the ball on the court. Don't try, just see. What may be hard is to keep your focus on the ball for an entire point, game, or match, and this, like any other skill, will need practice.

How do you know if you are seeing the ball well? This requires awareness. Are you able to answer these questions with absolute certainty?

- Am I really consciously seeing the ball all the way from my opponent's racket?

- Am I really focusing on the ball as my ball crosses the net and bounces up to my opponent's racket?

- If someone were to ask, could I tell them whether the ball was spinning fast, slow, or medium as it was coming to me and after I hit?

- Have I ever seen a ball that has no spin? Those balls should stick out like a sore thumb because they are so different from the rest.

- Am I able to see the ball spinning all the way to the blur of my racket when it makes contact with the ball?

You need to be able to answer these questions beyond a shadow of a doubt. If you find yourself saying that "I think" the ball was spinning slowly, then you didn't see it. If you really saw it you would say without a doubt, "Yes, I saw that one."

When I am giving a student a lesson for the first time, I usually start out by having them see the ball. I explain completely that I don't want them to think about their strokes or to think about hitting the ball into the court and instead want them to just focus on seeing the ball all the way to their racket and all the way back over the net to their opponent's racket.

After rallying with them for a few minutes, I then ask them if they saw the ball very well. Most of them will say that they did, and many times they will say that they saw the ball better than they ever had in the past. It is then that I give them "my little test." This test is the best way for me to tell if they are seeing the ball the way I want them to.

Here is what I say before I do the test with them. I say that I am going to give them every hint in the book so that they can get the "correct" answer to this test. I tell them that I will be hitting four balls to them, two to their forehand and two to their backhand. I will hit the balls as easy as I can (I stand at the net so that I can hit the ball really easy). I tell them that all four balls will have the identical spin, and I want them to tell me what direction the ball is spinning all the way from my racket to their racket. I tell them the three "key" words that practically give away the answer. Those words are "all the way" from my racket to your racket.

When I do the test, I hit the ball as easy as I can and I always use new balls so it is easier to see the spin of the ball. Would you believe that 98 percent of my students couldn't correctly tell me how the ball is spinning? I even give them another chance after explaining to them again the three key words, and they still don't get it right. Once I tell them how the ball is spinning and I hit them more balls, they see it immediately. The point I am making with this test is that people think they are seeing the ball well when really they are not.

Let me tell you a true story. I gave this test to a friend of mine who came up from California to play doubles with me in the National Indoor 60s tournament in Seattle. His name is Ken Stuart. Back in the old days, Ken was a world-class player. He is still a great player today, even though we have both aged a little. After I told Ken about watching the ball all the way to his racket and after we hit a few balls so he could get somewhat comfortable with focusing on the ball, I gave him the test. Well, he was one of the 2 percent who got it right the first time.

Because it was so easy for him, I think he thought that I was exaggerating about how many people got this test wrong just to make him feel good. Anyway, he went back home, and about three weeks later he called me and said that he gave my test to 10 or so other players, and all of them got it wrong. He now knows how special it was that he was able on the first try to see how the ball was spinning the way it needs to be seen. Did I tell you that when he could see the ball well, he really noticed the difference in how well he played?

Ken is the owner of the Palisades Tennis Club in Newport Beach, California, so if you ever get down there, give him a call and tell him that you would like to play at his club. His staff has a terrific way of matching you up with a player of your own level. If you get a chance to play there, you will see one of the best-run tennis clubs in America.

Are you wondering by now what the correct answer to my test is? Since I am not there to give you the test in person, I want you to try to give yourself the test. It won't be the same, but I am hoping that you will get the idea, not only about how you may not be seeing the ball as well as you could, but how really, really critical seeing the ball accurately is to your playing.

Here is what I want you to do. Please don't go and get the answer to the test yet. Wait until after the next time you play. Really work on seeing the ball as it comes to you, and notice which way it is spinning. After you get home, go to the super secret page on my tennis Web site (www.maxtennis.com/secret_answer.htm) and read about the test. On this page you will get all the answers to how the ball is really spinning as well as all the answers to the universe. It is absolutely critical that you go to this secret page because you will find information there about seeing the ball that you won't find in this book.

Seeing the ball the way I have described above and on my secret page may be a challenge for you. It took me years to get good at it, but when you really know you are seeing the ball, you will absolutely see a difference in your game. Some of the benefits of seeing the ball really well will be fewer miss-hits, more consistency, and more relaxed strokes. You will also begin to experience what it means to get your conscious mind out of the way and let your other than conscious mind direct your body.

Here are some games you can play that will help you to focus on the ball.

Play the bounce-hit game as taught in Tim Gallwey's *The Inner Game of Tennis*. Every time the ball hits your racket or your opponent's racket, say out loud or to yourself "hit." Every time the ball bounces on the ground, say out loud or to yourself "bounce." Check to see if you are saying "hit" with a relaxed voice or a tense one. And check to make sure that you are saying these words exactly when it is happening and not before or after.

Another game to play is to say out loud or to yourself what direction the ball is spinning. When you hit the ball, say what direction it is spinning as it is going over the net and again when the ball is coming back toward you. *Don't forget to consciously see the spin after the bounce.* And we all should know what direction the ball is spinning then, right?

Here is one more game to play. Watch the trajectory of the ball as it comes to you and as it goes back to the other side. Ask yourself whether the ball is still rising, has reached its peak, or is dropping when you hit it. Do the same when your opponent is hitting the ball.

As you learn to let go and just see the ball the way I describe above and in the Mental Game Core Principles, you will see amazing things begin to happen. If nothing much happens, then maybe you are just not seeing the ball properly and you will need to contact me.

If you want to get a visual picture of what it looks like when someone sees the ball all the way to contact, watch Roger Federer's head as he makes contact with the ball. He sees the ball better than any other professional I know of.

The final thing to understand about seeing the ball is that even though it is your conscious mind that is seeing the ball, you want to have your other than conscious mind make it happen. This means that, for example, when you read these words, you are not trying hard to read, you just do it. Do the same for seeing the ball. Just see it.

Now go see the ball and play the mental game.

Lesson #3 - The Power of the Breath

After seeing the ball as described in Lesson #2, the second most important thing to focus on is your breathing. This is because focusing on your breathing keeps the upper body more relaxed, thereby allowing your body to hit the ball better.

If any of you have taken a yoga class, you will know that breathing is a big part of getting the full benefit from it. Tennis is no different except that you will be using the breathing to stay in the here and now, as well as using it to help you learn how to keep your "conscious mind" out of the way. And, like yoga, working with your breathing, helps you relax properly.

The breathing is the most important part of the relaxation package (I will discuss the full relaxation package in Lesson #4), and you will need to work on it as much as on seeing the ball. In the Mental Game Core Principles, I talked a little about how to breathe but not about some of the practical ways to work on it. Here I will go into more detail.

Up until now, I have always told my students that the jury was still out as far as the "best" way to breathe, because I have always had difficulty allowing my breathing to be the way I felt it should be. Well, I think the jury may have arrived at a verdict.

The next time you play, begin by just being aware of your inhales and exhales as you are hitting the ball back and forth. Check to see if you are holding your breath when you make contact with the ball. Without this ability to consciously pay attention to yourself breathing, it will be difficult to work on changing your breathing in the way I describe below.

When you watch the pros play, you will hear some of them actually grunt out loud as they hit the ball. If you notice closely you will hear that they start this grunt or forced exhale as or after their racket makes contact with the ball. I don't think this way of breathing is as helpful as some other ways since it does little to relax their upper body, but at least they are breathing, and this is much better than holding their breath.

Once you have the ability to pay attention to your breathing, you can start working on the quality and rhythm of it. Here is what I consider to be the most effective and natural breathing pattern while hitting the ball.

Start your exhale before, as, or just after the ball bounces on your side as the ball is coming to you. This exhale should be a sigh that is long, slow, and relaxed and should continue well through contact with the ball. At the same time, of course, you are consciously seeing the ball all the way to the blur of your racket. You don't have to concern yourself with your inhales as I guarantee that you will do it.

Exhaling as you hit is a very natural way to breathe, so all you have to do is start your exhale before you hit the ball, make it smooth and relaxed, and make it longer than usual. It doesn't get any easier than that.

When you are at the net, you will notice that your breathing will have to be a little quicker. You will need to start your exhale just before, as, or just after the ball hits your opponent's racket and allow it to continue well through your hit. Do this, and you may see some amazing things happen with your volleys.

When your opponent is at net, it is also a little trickier because the ball is coming back sooner than normal, and you will have to start your exhale before you make contact with the ball.

Again, while you are working with your breathing, you still need to be focusing on the ball all the way to the blur of the racket. However, you may want to forget about seeing the ball for a while and just work on the breathing part. After you have spent some time with the breathing, you must then see if you can do both at the same time. Achieving both the correct breathing and seeing the ball at the same time, and without judgment, is the ultimate focus and leads to playing in the zone.

One of the ways I help myself pay attention to my breathing is to make a little sound (always a relaxed sigh) as I exhale. It is not a grunt, and no one else can hear me, but I can hear it inside my head.

The breathing will be a little different on your return of serve (see Lesson #14 for more info). You should be starting to exhale just before your opponent hits the ball. But the exhale is still a long, relaxed sigh and continues well through your hit. This way your upper body has a better chance to stay relaxed even when your body has to move quickly to react. This is especially important when playing someone with a big serve.

When you are serving you will also start the long, relaxed inhale before you make contact with the ball. And again, continue to exhale well through contact. You may also find that you will be able to see the ball to the blur of the racket that much easier.

The important points to remember are that no matter what shot you are hitting, the exhale should always be very relaxed (like a sigh) and that you start it before making contact with the ball and continue it long past contact.

Breathing was the last part of the inner game that I worked on. I didn't work on it very much in the beginning because I just could not let go enough to focus on both breathing and seeing the ball. However, once I did get serious about doing both (as described in the Mental Game Core Principles), my game started to really improve.

Doing both is not easy. It takes a lot of work and a lot of letting go. Please don't let that keep you from working on your breathing.

The obvious way to work on it is to just hit balls and see if you can pay attention to your breathing and for the moment forget about seeing the ball. If you are just playing a practice match, you can do it then also. However, if you are playing a match that is important to you and can't yet focus on both the ball and your breathing, I would rather have you just focus on the ball. I guess what I am trying to say is that when playing an important match, it is not the time to practice the way you breathe, but it is the time to have your breathing be as relaxed as possible, even if you can't consciously focus on it.

Another way to work on breathing (you can even do this in a game) is to play two points or rallies just paying attention to yourself exhaling. This means from the time the first point starts to when the second point ends and includes the time between points. And, of course, any thought of trying to see the ball, trying to hit the ball into the court, or trying to stroke it a certain way needs to be eliminated. If you happen to see the ball well at the same time, that would be wonderful and an added bonus.

Then play two points just seeing the ball. Again, make sure that you are focusing on the ball from the time the first point starts to the time the second point ends. Likewise, if you happen to feel yourself breathing at the same time, that is better.

Then see if you can pay attention to both your exhaling and seeing the ball for two points.

The ultimate goal here is to program the other than conscious mind to have the breathing be very relaxed. Just as when you are seeing the ball and the time comes to play the game, you need to get the conscious mind out of the way and again let your other than conscious mind keep your breathing relaxed.

35

Lesson #4 - Relaxation: Why This Is So Critical

Just about every time you miss the shot and it feels like you took a "bad" stroke or it feels awkward on a hit, you can pretty much narrow the problem down to a relaxation issue.

What do I mean by relaxation? When playing tennis, being relaxed properly means using only those muscles that are needed to execute the shot and using the right amount of tension. The problem is that no one knows exactly which muscles those are. The good news is that your other than conscious mind does, or it will learn. It is not, as one of my students thought for a while, the relaxed way you feel after or during a massage. This proper amount of relaxation and tension is demonstrated when we watch the professionals play and we say, "They make it look so easy."

When we try hard to do something (especially the first time and when learning any new physical skill), we use so many more muscles than we need to and often with much more tension. And we wonder why it takes so long for that new skill to become easy and second nature.

When I am teaching a student a different way to stroke the ball, many times he or she will have a death grip on the racket. I have to tell them that this is not a weight-lifting class and the racket does not weigh 1,000 pounds. The student also often feels that this new way of stroking is not natural or feels funny because they are so used to trying very hard.

Much of what I am doing is having my students discover only the muscles that are needed when hitting a particular stroke. I accomplish this by having them experience relaxing some part of their body starting with their grip and wrist.

Here is one of the little secrets of why relaxing works so well. When you are relaxing and not trying to control your body with your conscious mind, your body falls under the supervision of your other than conscious mind and it can then take control of your stroke using only the necessary muscles. Your other than conscious mind will also figure out exactly how to time the ball perfectly and what angle the racket must be at to hit the ball the way you want. If the body doesn't know, by keeping your conscious mind out of the way and keeping it from trying to control your body, your body will learn that much faster.

So, how do you work on using only the muscles you need, and how do you know if you are doing this? There are some signs that you can watch for. When you hit a ball and you feel awkward or the stroke feels hard to do, it means you are too tense somewhere in your body. If you have worked with my Mother of All Stroke Tips (see Lesson #40) and you are unable to keep your balance as you are holding, then you know you are too tense in your legs. If you have ever paid attention to what your face is doing when you hit the ball, you may notice that it is not relaxed and you are "making a face". That means you are too tense (maybe even holding your breath) and trying too hard.

Speaking of the face, let me tell you about Roger Federer. He does two things better than any other top pro that I am aware of. The first is that he must be seeing the ball as I discuss in Lesson #2. You can see his head follow the ball to his racket, and his head stays at that point for a period of time longer than any other player I have seen. You will see most other pros move their head to their racket, but not even close to how well Federer does it.

The second thing that Roger does that no other top pro even comes close to doing is what he does with his face. Or maybe I should say what he doesn't do with his face. In every picture I have seen of Roger hitting the ball, his face looks relaxed, and sometimes it looks like he may be exhaling gently. Even in pictures where he is obviously straining to get to the ball his face is relaxed. In every picture I have seen of other pros (male or female), you can see tension in their faces. What this means to me is that Roger is truly allowing his body to hit the ball and is not using any other muscles or is not trying to control his body consciously when he hits the ball. This is why in my opinion Roger will be (maybe already is) the greatest player the world has ever seen and will be on top for a long time to come.

OK, back to how to work on the relaxation issue. When you feel you are too tense somewhere, you first have to isolate where in the body the tension is located. Here are some of the areas, in order of importance, that seem to be common to most players.

- Breathing — holding the breath as you hit the ball or a tense exhalation (see Lesson #3)
- The grip and/or the wrist (see Lesson #11)
- The face
- Your legs
- Your left hand (your right hand if you are left-handed)
- Your left ear (OK, maybe I am being a little ridiculous)

Once you have determined what area you think may be tense, then all you need to do is pay attention to that area when you are hitting the ball. For example, if you think that your grip or your wrist is too tight, then pay attention to your five fingers as you hit the ball. If you use a two-handed backhand, pay attention to all 10 fingers as you hit. With this awareness you will discover the ability to become more relaxed.

At the same time you are working on relaxing by paying attention to some part of your body, it is critical that you refrain from trying to do anything about the tension. The trying leads to more tension. Let your other than conscious mind figure out how to hit the ball into the court using only the muscles that are truly needed, and get your conscious mind out of the way.

As you begin to be able to let go of all the other muscles you don't need when you are hitting the ball, your strokes will become natural and so much easier. Your game will improve, and you will find that you have more endurance because you are using so much less physical effort. I am sure that at times when you have played you have hit a shot that felt absolutely effortless. When this happens, you will know that you are in the state of perfect relaxation. This is what you are striving for. And, all this "letting go" leads to "playing in the zone."

Lesson #5: What about Listening?

Let me tell you a story. I have a good friend who is a Buddhist and one day we were talking and I asked him how he practiced being one. He said that there were a lot of meditations that he did and I asked him to give me an example. He said that he would just meditate and listen to all the sounds around him with no thoughts or judgments, but just being aware of them.

I thought that would be an interesting idea for when I am playing tennis as it would keep me in the here and now and keep my mind calm and clear. I had not done any listening on the court before. I had not been able to play for about 4 months because of an elbow injury, but I thought that I would just listen for the ball hitting the ground and hitting my racket when I got back into playing.

Before I was able to play again, I read Ron Waite's latest article on the Tennis Server web site (see Lesson #46) and lo and behold he talks about listening on the court. Go to this link on my web site to read his article called "Listen to Your Game" (www.maxtennis.com/articles.htm). I would strongly suggest that you read it. He has already had a lot of experience in listening. It is all about letting go and having a calm mind when you play, and I really believe listening when you play will help.

After I started playing again, I began to listen to the sound of the ball hitting the ground and the ball hitting the racket on both sides of the court. If you have done the bounce-hit exercise that I explained in Lesson #2, then this concept of listening is very similar except that you are hearing the ball instead of saying "bounce" or "hit". Of course, you will want to see the ball at the same time. Anyway, I have found it a very calming way to stay in the here and now as well as a technique to learn how to further let go of consciously trying to control your play.

As with some of the other drills and ideas that work on letting go, I don't believe that you will want to do this in a match that is important. You may use it when you are playing practice matches as it will be a good test for you to see if you can let go of your strokes and everything else enough to still hear the ball and see the ball at the same time. As always, the ultimate way to play the mental game is to use the "Core Principles."

Lesson #6 - How to Deal with Being Nervous

You just can't stop being nervous until you deal with the cause. Players get nervous for a reason. See if any of these possible reasons apply to you:

- Are you worried about losing?
- Are you making the match too important?
- Are you worried about playing badly?
- Are you worried about letting someone else down?
- Are you worried about any other issue?

All of these possible reasons boil down to wanting to win. You don't have to worry about winning or losing, because if you play better than your opponent, you will win (see Lesson #1). Just focus on the "Core" principles and you will be playing as well as you are able to.

You also have to let go of making the match important. When you make the match important, you will tense up, try too hard and thereby not play as well as you could. Remember, this is not life or death. It is just a game. Enjoy it.

Use the Mental Game Core Principles, and it will be impossible for you to be nervous when you are on the court because you will be playing a different game. You will be playing the mental game, which will help you play your best, and if that best is better than your opponent, then you will win. If you don't win, you will need to practice more on your weaknesses and maybe even on letting go.

Lesson #7 - Play at the Top of Your Game Every Time

Obviously, you cannot expect to play the best tennis you have ever played every time you are on the court. Sometimes your body just doesn't work very well. This can happen if you are tired, sick, or if your body is just out of sorts.

But what you can expect is that whatever condition your body is in, you can play the very best in that moment. Even if you start at a lower than normal level of play, you can and should be able to improve as the match continues.

There are some specific things to be aware of that can creep into your mind and will need to be addressed. The first one is judgment of your play. Here is a really good way to know if you are judging something -- if at any time you react verbally, mentally, or physically to a missed shot, then that is the sign that you are judging your shots and trying too hard. Once you are aware of these judgments, just let go of them and get back to using the Core Principles. You may find yourself playing really well again.

Lesson #8 - How You Can Turn Your Game Around If You Start to Play Badly: The One-Minute Method

Actually, it takes less than a minute. When you change sides and you are sitting down, take a deep breath, do a relaxing exhale (sigh), clear your mind, and reprogram what you want to do. This, of course, means letting go of all other thoughts and then refocusing on using and only using the Mental Game Core Principles. Are you getting the picture as to how you can play and win the Inner Game?

Lesson #9 - Why You Miss Shots and How to Fix Them on the Spot

If your strokes are solid and you miss a shot, it is my contention that it is due to the conscious mind getting involved, which in turn causes the body to tense up and then produces a physical stroke error. And even if your strokes are not as good as you would like, I still believe that 90 percent of the errors you make are when the conscious mind gets into the picture.

If you pay attention to where your focus was when you missed a ball, you may see a pattern. The questions you need to ask yourself are:

- Did I consciously see the ball all the way to the blur of my racket?
- Did I consciously feel my exhalation? If so, did I hold my breath as I made contact with the ball, and was my exhale really relaxed before and after contact with the ball?

If you answered "no" or "I don't know" to the above questions, then just go back to using the Mental Game Core Principles.

If you missed the ball long (always if you miss it long by three feet or more), it will most likely be because your grip and/or wrist was too tight or you were holding your breath.

Imagine or visualize that from now on you will relax your grip a little more and make your breathing more relaxed (especially the exhale). If you missed the ball long because the ball was hit too high over the net, take the time to imagine or visualize that from now on your body will hit the ball lower.

If you missed the ball in the net, it will most likely be because your arm was too tense on the backswing. This keeps the racket head too high and doesn't allow your racket head to get below the ball. Imagine or visualize that from now on you will relax your arm and wrist as this will let the racket head get lower. Also, imagine or visualize that from now on your body will hit the ball at least a foot over the net.

If you missed the ball just a little out, you would ask yourself how well you were seeing the ball to the blur of the racket, as not seeing it well is the most likely reason you missed. Imagine or visualize that from now on you will allow your eyes to follow the ball all the way to the blur of the racket.

Sometimes the above solutions don't work because you are just not able to focus. That is because there is something else going on. So, how do you fix it? Just knowing what mental error you made and reprogramming it is only half the answer.

You must then look beyond simply trying to focus more and deal with the other side of the issue. Here are two questions you will need to find answers for:

- What is causing you to lose your focus on the ball or on your breathing?
- What is causing your grip and/or wrist to be too tight?

You will need to become aware of your individual cause factors because once you know the answers to these two questions and address them, you can get back to successfully focusing on the ball and your breathing.

Here is an example of what I am talking about and how it works.

If you were just walking down the street, I do not believe that your grip, your wrist, and/or your breathing would automatically tense up. The reason is obvious. Nothing is going on that would cause it. But if you were walking alone down a dark alley late at night, you just might be a little tense if you heard a noise. So, there has to be a cause. When we are on the tennis court (until we become more aware of our thoughts), the cause of our tension may be out of our consciousness.

Ask yourself these questions as they will help bring the causes into your awareness:

- Are you trying to win?
- Are you trying to "not lose"
- Are you trying to hit the ball into the court (as opposed to letting your body do it)?
- Are you trying to make a perfect stroke?
- Are you trying to make a particular shot?
- Are you trying to direct the ball to a certain spot on the court?
- Are you trying to hit a winner?
- Are you trying to hit the ball hard?
- Are you trying too hard to see the ball?

- Are you judging how you hit your ball in any way?
- Are you thinking about anything else that is outside of tennis?

A "yes" to any of these questions will tell you what is keeping you from focusing properly and may be causing you to tense some part of your body in such a way that will make you miss more than you should.

The final action you must take to "fix" these issues is to clear your mind, take a deep breath, do a relaxing exhale, let go of (release) any "yes" question issues, and refocus on the ball and on your breathing. In other words, use the Mental Game Core Principles.

You can also talk to yourself, visualize or feel yourself hitting the ball perfectly into the court, making sure that you have eliminated any of the cause factors. You should do this especially if you are missing the same shot over and over again. You don't have time to say to your opponent, "Hang on for a couple of hours while I go practice on the ball machine", but you can spend a few seconds and reprogram yourself so that you can get back to using your Core Principles. You will amaze yourself on how well this works when it is done properly. The use of the Beach CD (see the information at the back of this book) will also help you reprogram and utilize the core principles if you are having difficulties.

You will use this process over and over again until you get it right. Based on my experience, this reprogramming process will continue for the rest of your life because even if you become the greatest player the world has ever seen, you will still miss shots.

This is what makes this mental approach so much fun, as you will be forever learning about yourself, growing, improving, and experiencing yourself.

And you will enjoy playing so much more.

Lesson #10 - If You Get Angry at Yourself and Don't Know How to Stop

Hopefully you know that getting angry with yourself is usually unproductive. Why you get angry with yourself is pretty easy to understand. You get angry because you have tried to do something over and over again and you still are making the same mistakes or you are expecting a different outcome.

When you miss an easy shot, for example, you tell yourself that you should have been able to hit that ball into the court, especially because it was so easy. So the next time you get an easy ball, you try even harder, using your conscious mind to hit it in, and because you have tensed up more by trying harder, you miss it again and get even more upset with yourself.

The obvious answer to this is for you to let go of trying to hit the ball into the court and let go of judging yourself or caring if you miss. I know this may be a little difficult, not only to accept, but also to understand why letting go of judgments helps you hit the ball into the court. However, it does work, and it is a really important part of the mental game.

You first need to know who is hitting the ball. It is not you. It is your body that is being directed by your other than conscious mind. When you (your conscious mind) try to control your body, your body won't function properly all the time, especially when the match gets tight. This is because you (your conscious mind) do not know exactly what muscles to use, what the angle of the racket must be, what the perfect timing of the shot is, etc.

Your body, however, knows more about how the ball needs to be hit. And if it doesn't, it will learn better and faster without you or your conscious mind trying to control it. You must work on getting your conscious mind out of the way. Your conscious mind's job is to set the goals for your body and then step out of the way. We accomplish this by relaxing, seeing the ball, breathing, and letting go of everything else. In other words you will use the Mental Game Core Principles.

There are two ways to quickly release your anger so you can get back to where you want to be. The first is The Sedona Method" (see www.sedona.com or follow the link found on my Web site, www.maxtennis.com/non_tennis_links.htm). I read The Sedona Method book first, and then I got the tapes and have found them to be really helpful. I have since recommended this method to some of my friends, and they all have gotten a great deal of help from it. What I like about it is that it is really, really simple, takes only a minute, and gives you results immediately. A bonus is that you can use The Sedona Method for releasing any emotional issues you may have in your day to day living.

The second way is to remember to lighten up and have fun. Remember that tennis is supposed to be a fun game, and no matter how good you get, you will still miss some balls. Even easy ones. When you play the mental game, you will miss fewer balls, which will, in turn, make it easier to enjoy the game.

Lesson #11 - When You Miss a Shot

When you miss a shot, you usually miss it in one of three ways: long, wide, or into the net. All three of these can and should be addressed as a non-stroke issue (see Lesson #9). If you miss when you are practicing your strokes, there may be a stroke component in why you miss, but if you miss when you are playing points (which means you are in a match), the following concepts should be applied.

The following corrections may be done when you miss only once. However, if there is a pattern as to where you are missing the ball (and two times missing the ball in the same place is a pattern), then you must address the issue immediately. Don't wait until the match is over and then say, "Boy, I sure missed a lot of shots long." Or "My backhand down the line wasn't working today." These need to be addressed on the spot.

When the Ball Goes Long

Any time you hit the ball long, it is a relaxation issue, not a stroke issue. The first and easiest thing to do is *imagine or visualize that from now on* you will relax your grip and your wrist a little bit more when you make contact with the ball. Secondly, if you missed the ball long because your ball cleared the net too high, then along with the first correction, take the time to *imagine or visualize that from now on* your ball will clear the net by one to two feet. And thirdly, since it is a relaxation issue, you may want to check your breathing to make sure you are not holding your breath at contact with the ball and that your exhalation is very relaxed. In all the suggestions above, after you have "reprogrammed" yourself, let it go and get back to seeing the ball and exhaling before and after you hit the ball (Core Principles).

When the Ball Goes into the Net

This is also a relaxation issue and not a stroke issue. The way to fix this is to relax your arm and wrist so that your backswing can get lower automatically and without effort. This will allow your arm and racket head to swing up to the ball so that the ball goes over the net. In addition, *imagine or visualize your ball* going one to two feet over the net. After you have reprogrammed yourself, let it go and get back to seeing the ball and exhaling before and after you hit the ball (Core Principles).

When the Ball Goes Wide

I have found that when I hit the ball wide, it is because I have tried too hard to hit the ball down the line or cross-court, and as a result, I was unable to see the ball to the blur of my racket. So, in this case, you may need to let go of your effort to direct the ball (relax) and make seeing the ball and your breathing more important. As in the previous situations, *imagine or visualize your ball* landing in the spot you want it to, and after you have reprogrammed yourself, let it go and get back to seeing the ball and exhaling before and after you hit the ball (Core Principles).

Lesson #12 - When You Miss-hit the Ball on Your Racket or When You Hit the Ball Off-center

One or both of the following usually cause you to hit the ball off-center:

- Your grip and your wrist are too tight, usually at impact.
- You are not seeing the ball all the way to the blur of your racket.

If this happens often, you will need to spend some time paying attention to your grip and your wrist at impact and know that you want them to be more relaxed. Tim Gallwey (*The Inner Game Of Tennis),* says that you should hold your racket like you would hold a bird -- tight enough that the bird can't get away, but not so tight that you would squash it.

Seeing the ball is critical, but if you still try hard to hit the ball in the center of the racket, you may still hit it off-center. I don't think there is a person alive whose conscious mind really knows how to hit the ball on the center of the racket. But the body knows, and it will learn how to do so if given the chance. That is why the grip and the wrist must be relaxed at the same time as you see the ball.

By relaxing more, you are giving your body the chance to learn where the center is. There is also a chance that tension held in the upper body due to holding one's breath is a factor. So, check that out with yourself.

I have helped many players who used to miss-hit the ball learn how to hit it more on the center by having them trust that their bodies knew more than they (their conscious minds) did. You develop this trust by letting go or relaxing some part of your body more.

Lesson #13 - How to Make the Ball Go Where You Want It to Go

The principle of hitting the ball where you want it to go is pretty simple, as you will see when you read this lesson. Still, it does take practice figuring out what I mean by "knowing." As you work on these mental game lessons, it will become easier for you to understand what this means.

Think about when you are warming up. You just know that you want to hit the ball down the middle, and without thinking very hard, if at all, you just do it. The same applies when you are hitting your balls cross-court, down the line, or anywhere else. It is simply knowing where you want the ball to go and then just doing it. Trying hard, thinking hard, making it important, or trying to consciously direct the ball won't work in the long run or when you are under pressure. The best way to achieve this knowing and therefore hit the ball where you want it to go is to see the ball all the way to the blur of your racket and trust that your other than conscious mind will direct your body.

Obviously, if you have not developed the skill of accurately hitting the ball to the corners (or anywhere else) to your satisfaction, then you must spend more time practicing using the drills found in Chapter 5. And while you are practicing, keep in mind this concept of knowing.

Lesson #14 - How to Hit the Return of Serve into the Court

Hitting the return of serve is a little different from hitting a normal ball. This is because you have the chance to get yourself together before you have to hit the ball. Once the point has started, you cannot stop and say you are not ready. Because the serve is usually hit harder than a regular shot, you must also prepare yourself to be able to react quickly.

Here are the steps to allow your body to hit the return back into the court:

1. Take a few seconds to visualize where you want your return to go (see Lesson #32). Just before your opponent makes contact with the ball, start a long, relaxed exhale. Your exhale should continue well through contact with the ball. Since the time factor is so short, this should not be a problem. Once you have started your exhale, you really don't have to think about it just as long as you don't hold it. But it would be better if you can still be aware of it during your hit.

2. At the same time as you are starting your exhale, you will be focusing on the ball as it comes off your opponent's racket, and you will be looking to see the direction and speed but not really thinking about it or trying to guess which direction it will be hit. Just allow yourself to know how it is coming. Trying or thinking here is not required.

3. Now comes the critical part. You must see the ball spinning after the bounce and all the way to the blur of your racket. Even if you cannot actually see the ball spinning (because it is spinning so fast), you still must be focusing on it. You will be surprised at how many balls you can actually see, even if they are coming very fast. It is especially critical for you to be aware of seeing the blur of your racket as the ball makes contact with it.

4. If you find that you are still missing a lot of returns and you are feeling really rushed on your stroke, try moving back 3 to 6 feet. You will be amazed at what a few feet will do to your ability to hit the ball back into the court.

5. There is one more aspect to the return of serve that

needs to be addressed and that is the ideal position you need to be in when waiting to return the serve. The ideal position is one where every muscle is in a relaxed state just waiting to allow you to move in any direction quickly. I believe that this position is not the position that you commonly see.

Most players wait for the return in a "crouch" position. However, when they actually hit the ball they are hitting the ball standing straight (unless they have to lunge for it). Don't take my word for this. Just watch some players. I believe that starting in a more relaxed, upright position keeps you better prepared for not only hitting the ball, but also for moving more quickly to the ball. I do believe that it has been proven that relaxed muscles react faster than tense ones. You just need to find that state of relaxation. That means that you can work on relaxing your grip, wrist, arm, shoulders, and legs as you are waiting to hit the return.

Please notice that I have said nothing about trying to hit the ball into the court. At this point, you will trust that your body will, in fact, perform for you, and if the ball doesn't go into the court, your body will learn how to make it happen.

If you can do these 5 steps, you will be amazed at how many times you can hit the return back, even on the fastest serve, and you won't even know how you did it.

Here is the best way to practice your return of serve: you must have a willing opponent, which means that you can only do it in practice matches and not in tournaments. You can even do it in doubles if all four of you agree to practice it.

- The point cannot start until the return of serve has been returned into the court.

- If you missed the return on your backhand side, your opponent must then serve all serves to your backhand until you get it back into the court. If you missed the return on the first serve, then your opponent will serve another first serve. If that first serve is missed, then your opponent will serve a second serve, but it still must be to the backhand side until you get it back. If your opponent misses the second serve, he or she will keep serving until the ball is in play. This means that he or she cannot double fault. This way you get to practice until you get it right.

- If your opponent serves an ace, then the challenge for him or her is to hit another ace. If you miss the return on the first serve, then the challenge for the server is to hit two first serves in a row. If the server double faults, he or she will have a chance to practice a second serve. That way the server gets to practice also.

This drill will allow you to do the return of serve over and over without worrying about losing the point. It also takes the advantage away from the server, as the server doesn't get a free point just because he or she hit a good serve. It is a terrific way to work on one of the most important shots in tennis.

Questions To Ask Yourself While Practicing Your Return Of Serve:

- Am I really, *consciously* seeing the ball come off the racket as my opponent hits the ball?

- Is my exhale starting before my opponent serves the ball and continuing through my hit?

- Am I *consciously* seeing the ball spinning after the ball bounces and after I hit the ball, even if I miss?
- Is my body relaxed enough as I am waiting to hit the return?

If you answer "no" to any of the above, then you will have to let go of whatever it is that may be interfering with your ability to stay focused.

- Am I hitting the ball long?

If yes, try hitting the ball just a little easier. This means relaxing your grip and wrist a little as you hit the ball. Also, try standing back three to six feet if you are continuously hitting the ball long.

Be sure to read Ron Waite's article "Many Happy Returns" summarized on my Web site under "Tennis Articles – Outlined" and/or the full article located on my Web site under "Tennis Articles on the Mental Game" (See Lesson #46).

Lesson #15 - What To Do Between Points

If you did not miss the shot or you have won the point and are doing what I suggest in the Mental Game Core Principles, ideally you would continue seeing the ball and being aware of your breathing when the point is over and until the next point starts. This will keep you focused.

Some instructors say to focus on something neutral like the strings on your racket. I say why waste time focusing on something that is not going to help you play better? By keeping your focus on the ball and your breathing between points, you will be ready to see the ball, and your body will have a chance to be relaxed and ready for the next point.

If you become aware of negative or unproductive thoughts, just say, "cancel, cancel," and then change the thought into something more productive and focus again on the ball and your breathing. If you have hit a good shot, it is OK to thank your body (after all, it is your body who hit it) and ask your other than conscious mind to keep those shots coming. However, if you have missed the shot, then you may want to do the following.

If a thought comes to you about your stroke, then you can mentally reprogram the stroke by visualizing how you want to hit it. This does not mean that you think about what you are doing wrong. You can even take a practice swing doing the stroke correctly. *This practice swing must be absolutely perfect and must be a complete swing. This practice swing must include not only the perfect swing but also seeing the imaginary ball, breathing properly, and hitting the ball into the court.* **Please don't do what I see some people do -- actually take a practice swing using the incorrect stroke they just used when they missed the shot.**

After you have done this, let go of and forget about your stroke. Go back to seeing the ball and breathing, and let your other than conscious mind figure out how to make the stroke change.

If you are aware of missing a certain shot more than once, immediately visualize hitting the ball into the court to the spot you would have liked the ball to go, using a perfectly relaxed stroke, consciously seeing the ball perfectly, and having your body breathe properly. After you have done this, go back to seeing the ball and breathing as the next point begins.

If you are aware of missing the shot because of an error in seeing the ball or in breathing, again imagine or visualize yourself seeing the ball perfectly all the way to your racket and all the way to your opponent's racket with perfect breathing.

If you find that you are having difficulty with your focus, then you must begin to address the causes (see Lesson #9).

Ask yourself the following questions:

- Was I trying to hit the ball into the court?
- Was I thinking about hitting the ball to a particular place on the court?
- Was I trying to hit a winner?
- Was there anything else going on that would have kept me from seeing the ball all the way to my racket?

If your answer was "yes" to any of the above questions, just be aware that this way of thinking is going to interfere with you playing your best. So make your mental correction, let it go, and get back to focusing on the ball, breathing, and letting your other than conscious mind direct your body on how to hit your shots.

Lesson #16 - Choking

Any time you are in a close match and then you lose, you need to take a look at what happened as the end of the match approached. You need to ask yourself, "Did I lose the match because I missed easy balls, or did my opponent win the match by hitting winners or forcing me into errors?"

If you lost the match because your opponent played better than you at the end and you didn't miss balls that you were hitting earlier in the match, then the only conclusion as to why you lost is that he or she played better than you did on that day. You may want to figure out how your opponent played better, where he or she was hurting you, and where your weaknesses were, and then work on them.

On the other hand, if you missed easy shots or played worse than you did earlier in the match, then you "choked."

The good news is that you can learn to not choke.

Here are some questions you need to ask yourself:

- As the match got closer, did I think about winning?
- Did I have any thoughts about losing?
- Did I have thoughts that said, "All I have to do is hold serve" or "If I win this next game I will win the set or match"?
- Did I have thoughts that said, "I better not lose my serve" or "If I lose this next game I will lose the set or match"?
- Did I try hard to win or to hit the ball in the court?
- Did I try hard to "not lose"?

Any thought of winning (or losing) at this time of the match is death. Any thought of winning (or losing) at any time of the match is death. Trying hard to do anything, especially at this time of the match, is death.

What happens at this time is that you start to try harder, and therefore you start tensing up. As you miss more, you try even harder, you get more tense, and the cycle continues.

So, what do you do? You do the opposite. You relax more (this means that you are trusting your body to hit the shots), and you watch the ball better (without trying hard, of course) while you exhale properly and let your body play. The closer the match, the more you want to trust your other than conscious mind to make your shots. This means that you focus well, yet keep your conscious mind out of the way and keep it from controlling your shots. And, of course, this happens when you keep your body relaxed.

At the same time, your opponent is doing what you used to do. He or she is trying harder because at this time of the match he or she is thinking that winning every point is very important and therefore will most likely be the one tensing up and choking. I can't tell you how many times I have seen this happen when I get into a close match, and especially in a tie-breaker situation.

Lesson #17 – How to Warm Up for a Match

If you are going to play a match or a friendly game, your warm-up time will be the foundation you will build upon when the game actually starts. When the game does start, you will want to be able to continue playing as well as or better than you did when warming up.

I will address the warm-up for only the following two situations: one situation is when you are just playing a match for fun, and the other will be when you are warming up for a tournament match. Let's take the friendly match first, since you will most likely be playing more of these.

On the very first ball you hit, you should start by focusing only on the ball, making sure that you can really see it the way I have presented this in Lesson #2. Once you have gotten comfortable with seeing the ball, add the breathing component (see Lesson #3). If you are very comfortable with both the breathing and seeing the ball, then I would suggest that you start out on the first ball with both seeing the ball and the breathing.

After you get comfortable with seeing the ball and breathing, add some relaxation awareness. Start with feeling the grip and the wrist at impact to make sure they are relaxed. By now you should know the signs that tell you the grip needs to be relaxed a little more (see Lesson #11).

At the same time as you are feeling your grip and wrist, I would suggest that you incorporate the Mother of All Stroke Tips (see Lesson #40) and hold your follow-through. This will get you into a groove with your strokes.

All of these things should also be done with volleys, overheads and serves, and shouldn't take much time. When warming up your overhead, if you are playing with a friend who is willing, use the lob and overhead exercise found in Lessons #33 and #34.

When you warm up your serve, depending on how much time you have, use the following pattern:

- Hit a minimum of three first serves in a row to the backhand (right) corner.

- Hit a minimum of three first serves in a row to the forehand (left) corner.

- Hit a minimum of three second serves in a row to the backhand (right) side.

- Hit a minimum of three second serves in a row to the forehand (left) side.

- In your next three practice serves, hit one first serve to the right side, hit another first serve to the forehand side, and then hit a second serve to the backhand side.

- If you have enough time, repeat this in the ad court.

And, of course, while you are serving, you are seeing the ball to the blur of the racket and exhaling properly. When your opponent is practicing serving, you can practice seeing the ball spinning after the bounce as you catch it. This way you will be used to seeing the ball when the match starts.

When warming up for a tournament, there will be little difference from warming up for a practice match. You can do everything described in warming up for a practice match, except for two things. One of these is that you will do the warm up as described above for a practice match, only you will do it one to three hours earlier than your actual match. The second is that you may want to do a few easy placement drills like hitting cross-court, down-the-line drills, and you will want to serve a few more balls. You may even want to play a few points. Other than these additional items, this warm-up will be the same as the practice match warm-up. This practice should be only for 20 to 30 minutes.

When you actually get on the court to play your match, you usually get 5 to 10 minutes to warm up. During this warm-up, you will just be watching the ball and working with your breathing as if you were playing the match. You will have no thought of the stroke (except to relax it), and you will have the Core Principles in mind. This way, when the match starts, you will be ready.

Lesson #18 - If You Play Differently in Your Warm-up Than You Do When the Game Starts

First of all, you must understand what is so different. There are three differences when the game starts. One difference is that you will now want to do something with the ball other than hit it down the middle. The second is that your opponent will not be hitting the ball down the middle any more, and what he or she does with the ball affects your shots. And the third is that all of a sudden everything is more important. When you are just warming up, it doesn't matter if you miss the ball. You are not trying to aim your shots or even trying to hit the balls into the court (I hope). You are just hitting the ball down the middle.

If you really think about it, making the game important all of a sudden just because the game has started is the main cause of playing differently. Once the game starts, you must "trick" your conscious mind into thinking that the game is not any more important than the warm-up. Stop trying to aim or hit the ball into the court. Your body already knows how to do this. You did it in the warm-up. Stop trying to hit a perfect stroke. This is not the time for working on your strokes. Stop trying to win. Reprogram any thoughts you may have about losing. If you play better than your opponent, winning will take care of itself. And, most importantly, read and use the Mental Game Core Principles. They work. If you can do this, the only difference between the warm-up and when you start the game will be what your opponent does with the ball and the effect that has on your shots.

Lesson #19 - How to Play a Tie-breaker

Please read this lesson and the next one at the same time as both address pretty much the same issues.

In a tie-breaker, all of a sudden each point becomes very important. So, what do we normally do? We try harder. When you start to try harder, you start tensing up, and as you miss more, you try even harder and get more and more tense, and the cycle continues. *So, what do you do? You do the opposite.* You relax more (this means that you are trusting your body to hit the shots), and you see the ball better while you breathe properly and let your body play. The closer the match, the more you want to trust your other than conscious mind to make your shots. This means that you focus well yet keep your conscious mind out of the way so that it does not control your shots. And, of course, this happens when your body is relaxed. Your opponent will still be doing what you used to do. He or she will be trying harder (because winning every point is now very important) and will most likely be the one tensing up and choking.

I find that I will win 95 percent of the tie-breakers I play because I really relax and let go more at this time. When

I lose a tie-breaker, my opponent wins it. I don't lose it by missing "nothing" balls. And it is amazing how many times my opponent loses points that by all rights should be his.

Lesson #20 - How to Win When You Are Ahead (in a Game or Set)

If you find yourself losing after you have been ahead, you will need to ask yourself this question: "Is my opponent winning the points (hitting winners or forcing me into errors), or am I just missing shots?" If your opponent is winning the points, there is little you can do except to hit better balls so that he or she can't hit those winning shots. You may need to change your strategy.

However, if you are just missing shots, then there is something you can do. Here are some questions you need to ask yourself:

- Did I think about "winning"?
- Did I think about "losing"?
- Did I have thoughts that said, "All I have to do is win this next point" and/or "If I win this next point (game) I will win the game, set, or match"?
- Did I have thoughts that said, "I better not lose my serve" or "If I lose this next game I will lose the set or match"?
- Did I try hard to win or to hit the ball in the court?

<u>Any thought of winning (or losing) at this time of the match is death. Any thought of winning (or</u>

**losing) at any time of the match is death. Trying hard to do anything, especially at these times of the match, is death.**

What happens when these thoughts occur is that you start to try harder, and therefore you start tensing up, and as you miss more, you try even harder and get more tense, and the cycle continues. _So, what do you do? You do the opposite._ You relax more (this means that you are trusting your body to hit the shots), and you see the ball better while you breathe properly and let your body play. The closer you are to winning the match, the more you want to trust your other than conscious mind to make your shots. This means that you focus well yet keep your conscious mind out of the way so that it does not control your shots. And, of course, this happens when you keep your body relaxed. Your opponent will still be doing what you used to do. He or she will be trying harder (because winning every point is more important) and will most likely be the one tensing up.

If you have just read the last two lessons together, you have noticed that the solutions to both of these problems are the same. In fact, you may have noticed that I keep repeating the same things over and over. I am hoping that by my emphasizing these points, you can see how to overcome the unproductive patterns you have developed over the years. You would not be reading this had your solution (if any) worked. You need to reprogram your mind and adopt a different approach to these situations. When you are able to incorporate these ideas into your play, you will see that they really work.

Lesson #21 - How to Aim the Serve

This lesson is more than just how to aim. This is really about not missing your serve and/or about hitting a much higher percentage of your serves into the court. You won't have to worry or think about double faulting because when you take the time to visualize properly, you will not double fault. And you will find that you will be hitting many more first serves in, and with better accuracy.

The Full Visualization

The first thing to do is to pick out the exact spot, not a general area, on the court where you want your ball to bounce. Then follow *(visualize)* the trajectory back to where the ball would cross the net, look at the square (notice that the net is made up of little squares) the ball must pass over and imagine *(visualize)* the ball passing over this square (two to six inches for a first serve, about a foot for a second serve). Then follow *(visualize)* the trajectory back to where you are going to hit the ball with your racket, by starting the visualization again from the beginning to the end, *visualizing* seeing the ball on the toss, imagining *(visualizing)* seeing the ball to the blur of the racket with a perfect exhalation (starting before making contact with the ball and continuing long after), seeing *(visualizing)* the ball going over the square (two to six inches for a first serve, about a foot for a second serve) in the net, and hitting the spot on the court you have picked out.

When you go to actually serve, just "know" where you want the ball to go, see the ball all the way to the blur of the racket, start your breathing (use a very relaxed and long exhale) before you make contact with the ball, and continue to exhale long after. Trust your body to hit it where you want it to go, and/or let your body learn how. If you feel like you are doing everything right and the ball is not going where you want it to, or you notice that your body is not learning how to hit your target, then you may need to *relax* some part of your body.

One of the biggest "errors" my students make when I teach them this technique is they do not take enough time before each serve to do the process of visualizing justice. Remember, you have control of when you start the point when you are serving. So, be sure to take enough time before you serve to do this technique properly.

Another "error" my students make is to forget to do any visualizing at all when they are playing. You have to become aware of the fact that your first serve is not going in enough or you are double faulting a lot and then have the presence of mind to stop and use this visualizing technique.

This is a very powerful technique and as you work with this visualizing process, you will see your serve become more and more consistent and accurate. You can begin to hit more first serves in, even during a match, but you have to remember to use this process.

The Quick Visualization

The quick version of aiming the serve is to just pick the exact spot on the court, not a general area, you want the ball to hit.

When you go to actually serve, do the same as the full visualization. Just "know" where you want the ball to go, see the ball all the way to the blur of the racket, start your breathing (use a very relaxed and long exhale) before you make contact with the ball, and continue to exhale long after. Trust your body to hit it where you want it to go, and/or let your body learn how. If you feel like you are doing everything right and the ball is not going where you want it to, or you notice that your body is not learning how to hit your target, then you may need to *relax* some part of your body.

If you miss the ball long or into the net, you may want to take a moment to more formally visualize seeing the ball go two to six inches over the net. If you feel like you are doing everything right and the ball is not going where you want it to, or you notice that your body is not learning how to hit your target, then you may need to *relax* some part of your body.

While practicing your serve, use the following checklist:

- Am I *consciously* seeing the ball to the blur of the racket?
- Am I following the ball as it goes over the net? (You won't be able to see it spin, but you can focus on it.)
- Have I visualized the serve, including seeing the ball, as well as the speed, the stroke, and the exact path of the ball (two to six inches over the net) immediately before I serve?
- Am I allowing a long and relaxed exhalation just before and after I hit the ball?
- Am I relaxing my grip and/or my wrist enough as I make contact with the ball?
- Am I relaxing my arm enough as it goes through the swing?

A "no" answer to any of these questions means that you need to pay attention to that aspect, knowing that it needs to change.

I have one last thought about aiming your first serve that you may want to do once you see how accurate your serve can be using this technique. In the past when I chose the exact spot I wanted my first serve to go, I chose a spot about a foot inside the lines. I felt that extra foot would give me a margin of error. Not having a very hard serve, I got tired of having players return my serve even when I hit my target. When I put a road cone in the service box to aim at and when I was serving well, I found that I could hit the cone at least one out of ten times and often more than that. I had the thought that if my serve was that accurate (thanks to my body), I would change my exact spot to right on the lines. Once I didn't worry about the margin of error, my serve became much more effective because now I was able to hit ever so much closer to the lines. Even if your serve is not that fast, that extra distance closer to the lines really makes a difference.

Lesson #22 - When You Miss the First Serve

When I miss my first serve, I am aware that I either did not see the ball to the blur of my racket or did not breathe the way I wanted to.

So, I reprogram myself to consciously see the ball to the blur of my racket and to consciously exhale before and after I make contact with the ball. If I see a pattern in where I am missing, I will take the time to do a formal visualization on where I want the ball to go (see Lesson #21).

If the above doesn't work, then I will begin to relax some part of my body, starting with my grip and wrist at contact, then going to any other part of my body that may be tensing up and causing me to miss the serve.

Use the checklist found in Lesson #21.

Lesson #23 – About Hitting Winners

The concept of hitting winners is like the concept of winning. You are not to try to win; you are to find a way to play your best and let winning take care of itself. Likewise, you are not to try to hit winners; you are to just hit the ball where you want it to go using the appropriate power, and if it is a winner, so much the better.

When you try to hit winners, you will know by now that most likely you will not be watching the ball very well, nor will your breathing be relaxed. I also hope that you know by now that I am not talking about never hitting the ball hard. I am talking about just knowing when you need to hit the ball hard (the same as knowing where you want the ball to go), and if you place it well and your opponent can't get to it, then by its very nature it will be a winner.

And after you hit this great shot, be sure to pat yourself on the back, thank your body for hitting it and be sure to encourage it to keep hitting them. *Please resist the thought that you did it, as this will lead to trying. Also, please resist the urge to start trying to hit more and more winners.* Just keep your conscious mind out of the way and know that your body will do it for you. Believe me, it can and will.

Lesson #24 – About Your Weaknesses

Even the best players have weaknesses, but how you deal with them is always an interesting issue. I see a lot of people trying very hard to avoid their weaknesses. For example, the most obvious one is when I see players running around their backhands just for the sake of avoiding them. Or I see players practicing their forehands by the hour with no thought of hitting backhands.

From my way of thinking, if your backhand is weaker, you should be wishing that your opponent hit all the balls to your backhand. Likewise, if you have difficulty hitting down the line, you should be hitting down the line even if you miss and lose the point. Sometimes I even hit my weak shot when it is not the best time to do it from a strategy point of view just, so I can hit more of them.

In the above discussion, I am not suggesting that you practice your weakness if you are playing for money, playing in a tournament, or playing in any match where it is critical to win. But when you change the way you feel about your weaknesses and deal with them head on, this approach will lead to a much faster strengthening of those weaknesses.

Lesson #25 - Running and Hitting – How to Do It

I am not a biomechanics expert, but I do know some things about running and hitting. If you have observed yourself or other players when you/they are running hard for a ball, you may have seen a pattern when you or they miss the ball. I have observed in myself and others that most players miss the ball long. The next time you watch a game or when you play, take a look and see if this is true.

Anyway, the point is that when you run, you have the tendency to run hard with the lower body, and as a result the upper body follows suit. What must be learned is to run hard (but also relaxed) from below, but allow the upper body to be as relaxed as if you were standing still.

Easier said than done, you say. The way you can work on this is to really pay attention to your breathing when you are running fast for a ball, and make sure that you are not holding your breath and that your exhalation is as relaxed as possible before and after you hit the ball.

When I work on my running and hitting, I really work on relaxing my breathing as I hit the balls. And, of course, seeing the ball to the blur of my racket is also very helpful in allowing the upper body to be relaxed when running and hitting. Did you know that if you are able to breathe properly on a running ball, your face will be as relaxed as Roger Federer's? Just think. You can then say that you play just like he does. (ha ha)

You can practice using the method I talk about in Lesson #3 and play two points or rallies paying attention to your breathing, two points seeing the ball, and two points combining. Another good way to practice running and hitting is to start with an easy run to the ball to see if you can keep your breathing relaxed through the hit. Then see if you can still do this on harder and harder runs to the ball. Pretty soon it will be easier.

As critical as breathing is when running and hitting, so is the skill of seeing the ball to the blur of the racket, and it must be worked on until you have it mastered. If you really analyze how you have missed a ball when you have had to run hard for it, you will find out that you have made one or all of the three classic errors: holding your breath, not seeing the ball to the racket, or having some part of your body too tense.

Lesson #26 – Learn To Deal With Noise And Visual Distractions

Have you ever let the noise of an airplane distract you? How about a car horn honking or someone yelling about a missed ball on the next court? What about seeing a ball rolling in the back of the court and because you didn't see it in time to call a let, you lost the point because you let it distract you? All of these and any other distractions can really play havoc with your tennis if you let it.

Again, as in many of my lessons, the concept is pretty simple but it may take some time and practice. Here is what you do. Just acknowledge the distraction, know that it is part of life, no one is out to get you, and without judgment just let it go and go back to seeing the ball and feeling your breathing. Remember also, these distractions happen to both of you, but now you know how to deal with them. You can only hope that your opponent will still be bothered by them.

I can't tell you how many times in the past I have lost the point because I was distracted by a ball that rolled onto the back of either my side or my opponent's side. One day I thought enough is enough so when I played practice matches, I would never call a let if a ball came into the court. The only exception was if the ball actually rolled in front of us or if there was a danger of either of us stepping on it. With a little practice of letting it be OK for the ball to be there, staying with my breathing and seeing the ball, I found that I wasn't losing those points anymore. Do the same for any distraction that comes up. Remember, these distractions are also a part of playing.

Lesson #27 - The Wondering Technique

When you have a question and you don't know the answer, you can use the "Wondering Technique". This is another terrific concept I learned from Dave Dobson (see info on his audio CD at the back of this book). For example, if you are behind in the score and you can't figure out what strategy change you need, you would say to your other than conscious mind, "*I wonder* how I can change my strategy so that I will be more effective." Or you could say, "*I wonder* what I could do to play better." Then you just relax and let the answer come to you.

Here is the reasoning behind this technique. Back in the old days when we were on the phone and someone tried to call us, they got a busy signal. We didn't have "call waiting" then. There was no way that the person calling you could get through, and you didn't know that someone was trying to call you. Trying hard to think about what different strategy to use is like being on the phone, and when the answer does come, your answer will get a busy signal and not get through because your mind is too active. So just relax your conscious mind and let the answer come to you. With practice, this can be a very powerful tool.

Lesson #28 - How to Know If You Are Playing the Mental Game Properly

I assume that by now you have read all of the lessons on the mental part of tennis in this chapter and hopefully you have begun to put these lessons into practice. You may also be "sick to death" of hearing about seeing the ball, breathing, letting go, relaxing, and the core principles. I hope not. I go over and over these so many times because we have learned all of our lives to try hard, make it happen, beat your opponent, etc and it will take some serious effort to "correct" these thought patterns. With repetition, I am re-enforcing these new patterns of thought. You can see that there are not that many things you need to do to play the mental game. Using the Core principles when you play is really all there is to it. You just need to strip away all the unproductive thoughts that get in your way.

You now need to know if you are playing the mental game properly, or at least making progress.

Here are some questions you can ask yourself which will give you the knowledge that you are on the right track.

- Does your play improve during a match?
- Have you seen at least one ball to the blur of your racket when you are playing sets or matches?
- Have you felt yourself exhale properly for at least one ball during a match?
- Have you re-programmed any of your misses either in practice or in a match?
- Have you been aware of any unproductive thoughts and had the presence of mind to stop and re-program?
- Even if you are not able to focus very well, are you constantly re-programming yourself to see the ball on every point and working with letting go more and more?
- Are you making the mental game the most important thing to work on when you play? (I am talking about using the Core Principles.)

Any 'yes' answer to the above questions should tell you that you are on the path of playing the mental game. As I have said before, this is a lifelong process, and improvement in focusing and letting go will continue until you retire from the game, assuming that you work on it and make it important. When you work with this aspect of tennis, you will find that your enjoyment of the game will be greatly enhanced.

Chapter 3 – Strategy

Most of the strategy Lessons found in this book are singles oriented. However, some of these ideas can be adapted for doubles use and I have a whole lesson devoted to basic doubles strategy (see Lesson #39).

Lesson #29 – The Strategy of Consistency: The First and Last Resort

The whole idea of playing the game of tennis is to hit the ball into the court more times than your opponent. Depending on your level of play, using just the strategy of consistency may be what gives you the win. So, if your life depended on hitting the ball into the court, how would you go about doing it?

There are three obstacles to hitting the ball into the court. The first is that you must hit the ball over the net. OK, so how high do you think you should hit it? How about three to six feet over the net. That way you will have a pretty good margin of error.

The next obstacle is the baseline. When you hit the ball three to six feet over the net, you cannot hit the ball too hard; otherwise it will go long. So you must hit the ball fairly easy.

The third obstacle is the sidelines. The obvious way to overcome this is to hit the ball right down the middle.

So, by hitting the ball high over the net, fairly easy, and right down the middle, you will cut down drastically on missing the ball. Use this strategy if and when you start missing your regular shots. Then when you get your groove back and regain your focus, you can start to hit the ball harder and with more placements closer to the sidelines and the baseline (see Lesson #13).

Lesson #30 - The Three Major Weaknesses and How You Can Exploit Them

Most players have three major weaknesses. However, these weaknesses tend to disappear as the player advances in skill. Here they are:

1. *Backhands* – Again, the exception may be if the player hits a two-handed backhand. Then you need to pay closer attention to see if this is indeed weaker. And if the player's forehand and backhands are both good, you can make your determination on which side he or she hits harder and/or more accurately, thereby forcing you into errors more often.

2. *Running and hitting* is also a weakness. It is easier for you to hit the ball when it comes to you than when you have to run for it. The same is true for your opponent.

3. *Hitting the ball deep* is also harder for your opponent to hit back. Many times a deep ball will come back short or the player will miss it.

Of these three weaknesses, which one do you think is the easiest to exploit? If you said, "Hit to the backhand," you would be correct. It is easier to hit to one side of the court than it is to make someone run or hit deep. So, pound (this means hit a lot of balls to) the backhand side and wait for a relatively easy ball that you can hit to the forehand and make them run. And, of course, unless you are going for a sharp angle or drop shot, work on hitting all of your balls deep.

After you have hit to the forehand side to make your opponent run, hit the next ball to the backhand side again to make your opponent hit a running backhand. This way you can exploit two weaknesses within a single point.

You should be hitting anywhere from 2 to 10 balls in a row to the backhand before you make the shot to make your opponent run (especially if your opponent has a really good forehand). This way, when you do give your opponent a forehand, not only will you be making your opponent run, but they may just miss it because they have lost their groove and/or rhythm (see Lesson #38).

Lesson #31 - How to Determine If Your Opponent's Backhand or Forehand Is Weaker

When you are warming up, you can get a pretty good picture of which stroke is stronger or weaker. Be sure to hit enough balls to each side so that you have enough information to make a determination. If your opponent's forehand and backhand look the same, you will need to do some more investigating. When the game starts, assume that the backhand is weaker. If you find you are getting hurt by the backhand, change and begin hitting most of your balls to the forehand and see what happens. Use the same plan for determining weaknesses when your opponent is warming up volleys and overheads.

Lesson #32 – Why You Should Hit All Serve Returns Cross-court

When I talk here about hitting cross-court, I mean hitting all forehands (assuming you are right handed) to the left corner and all backhands to the right corner, no matter which side you are receiving on.

Here is my reasoning for returning the serve cross-court. It is an easier and more natural stroke to hit the ball cross-court and a key element of breaking your opponent's serve is just to get the return back in play, hopefully well enough that you don't give them a setup. By hitting the easiest and most natural shot, you will hit that many more returns back.

In addition, it is harder to hit a return down the line because when the ball is coming fast, you have less time to turn your body enough to make it an easy shot. If you are in the deuce court hitting a cross-court forehand, not only is the distance to the baseline longer, but you will also be hitting the ball over the low part of the net. The same is true in the ad court if you are hitting a backhand.

Here is another reason for hitting the return cross-court: If you think about it, breaking serve is rare. So by hitting the ball cross-court, you are attempting to do three things other than just getting it back. First, you are attempting to make your opponent hit a running ball (which is a weakness for most players or at least more difficult). Second, you are pulling your opponent wide and/or off the court. And third, you are attempting to get control of the point on the first hit. The nature of the serve gives the server an advantage because, assuming your opponent has a good serve, most of the time the server is in control of the point from the beginning. So, all you need to do is to string together a couple of good returns so you can take control and win the point. This will put that much more pressure on your opponent, and with some of his or her errors, you will have broken the serve.

Also, you won't have to think about where you are going to hit your return, as you have already planned it. This in itself is important because it will allow you stay that much more relaxed, and you will be able to concentrate on seeing the ball and breathing.

As for worrying that your opponent will know where you are returning the serve, believe me, most players will not have a clue. Even if they do, if you hit a good return, you will be making them run wide and you will be taking control of the point. I have played many good players and asked them afterward if they saw a pattern on my serve return, and about 98 percent of them said no, they didn't know where I was hitting it. Of course, everyone knows now, because I just told them.

My final point is that if hitting cross-court is good enough for the best players in the world, it should be good enough for us. In the 2005 U.S. Open Finals, I observed both Agassi and Federer hitting their returns of serves cross-court more than 95 percent of the time. They must have learned it from me (ha ha).

Lesson #33 - Where to Hit Your Lob and How to Practice It

Always hit your lob cross-court. This will give you the longest distance to hit, thereby giving you a greater margin of error. If you think back to when you have had to hit an overhead that has been hit cross-court, you will know how much harder it is. Yes, your opponent has more time to get to your lob because your lob has longer to travel, but he or she will have to run farther. Obviously, this idea applies to singles only. In doubles, lobbing over the net player is the place to lob.

How to Practice Your Lob

I will be willing to bet that you don't spend much time, if any, practicing your lobs and overheads. Most of the time when you are warming up your opponent's overheads, you just try to feed the lob to them so they can hit an easy overhead. Here is an easy way to practice both the lob and overhead if you have a willing partner who will do this drill with you when you are playing a practice match.

Hit the first ball to make your opponent hit a volley, then hit a lob on the return of that shot. When you hit your lob, do not try to just feed it to him or her. Go for the perfect lob cross-court. If your opponent hits an overhead back to you, hit your opponent another volley (not a lob), and then hit another lob if he or she returns your shot. Your opponent should be hitting overheads for winners. This way you both can warm up practicing what you would do in an actual match. *See the next lesson, #34, about why you want to hit your overhead as hard as you can.*

Here is my reasoning: using this drill, you can practice your lob every time you warm up, assuming you are playing with someone you know who wants to warm up this way. By only hitting a lob from a volley, you will be practicing hitting a lob like you would in a match. *When you hit your lob, make sure your breathing is relaxed, and you see the ball spinning all the way to the blur of your racket.* Since I consider the lob to be a "touch shot," relaxing more as you hit the ball is a must.

If you are hitting your lobs long, then you will need to relax your grip and your wrist just a little as you make contact with the ball. Pretty soon your body will learn the exact tension it needs to hit a good lob.

Lesson #34 —Why You Should Hit All Overheads as Hard as You Can

Let me tell you a story. Quite a few years ago, I was playing in a tournament on a slow court against a steady player who was fast on his feet. I felt I needed to go to the net because I couldn't win the points from the baseline, and he was tiring me out. But when I went to the net, he lobbed a lot, and I just tried to angle my overhead off. I quickly found out that didn't work. He just ran it down and hit an even better lob or hit a passing shot. Not only did I get very tired, I lost the match.

After the match, I got to thinking that if I hit my overhead as hard as I could, I could end the point then and there, and I wouldn't get so tired. I also thought that all I had to do was to hit my overhead five or six feet away from him and because my ball was going so fast he would not have time to get to it, and if he was able to get his racket on it, his shot would be weaker, and I would be able to really put the ball away on the next shot.

So, here is what happened. I started hitting my overheads as hard as I could, and I found from then on that I almost never missed my overhead, I almost always won the point on the first hit, and I was less tired because the points were shorter.

Obviously, you must use some common sense when hitting your overhead as hard as you can. That means that if you can just barely reach the ball, you cannot and should not try to hit it hard. To do so may hurt your arm or shoulder because of the awkward way you must hit the ball.

Hint: You still must see the ball spinning to the blur of your racket and allow yourself to exhale before making contact with the ball.

Lesson #35 - If You Get a Short Ball, Hit a Drop Shot

If you get a short ball, hit a drop shot and then close to the net to cut off any angle. Even if your drop shot is not really good, there are still a lot of advantages. In order for your opponent to hit his or her ball into the court, he or she must hit the ball easier because the distance to the baseline is shorter, and he or she must hit up on the ball in order to get it over the net. This will give you more time to react and hit a winner, but many times your opponent will just miss the ball or not even get to it.

If your opponent tries to lob, the same principle applies. Because the distance is shorter, your opponent must hit the lob more up and down and with a good touch. If he or she doesn't miss the ball long, you will have more time to run it down because the ball has to go at a much more vertical angle while you are running straight back.

After your opponent has figured out that you will drop shot a short ball, he or she will start moving in toward the net.

This is the time to hit your normal approach shot. Because your opponent is moving toward the net to get your drop shot, your normal approach shot will be more effective. Then keep mixing them up, and your opponent will never know what you are going to do.

Lesson #36 - When You Serve a Let Ball

When you serve a let on your first serve, serve the next first serve to the opposite side, and many times your opponent will miss the return. This doesn't work every time, but it has worked enough for me to use it.

Lesson #37 - When You Get Pulled out Wide

When you get pulled out wide and you know you will have trouble getting back into the court, hit the ball very hard. The idea here is that you are in trouble and you have to do something to prevent your opponent from hitting the ball for a winner. Maybe you are fast enough to get back into the court, but being an "old, slow guy," this works for me some of the time and is the only choice I have.

This is also a good time to lob, but if your opponent has a good overhead, you will lose the point anyway. You can also try to hit your ball high over the net (but not high like a lob) to see what your opponent will do. If your opponent moves in to the net, then this is also an easy shot for him or her.

So, hitting your ball really hard will make it more difficult for your opponent to make his or her shot. You should also try to hit the ball cross-court because it will be harder for your opponent to hit a change-of-direction ball and hit down the line.

Lesson #38 - A Basic Singles Strategy

For the explanation of this strategy, I assume that the backhand is the weaker side and that the player is right-handed. There are many variations to this that you can use depending on how your opponent returns the ball (patterns) and how he or she moves, but this is meant to be just the beginning step in the area of singles strategy. I will use the term "appropriate ball" throughout this lesson. Here is what I mean by this:

An *appropriate ball* is a ball you have hit so well that you have forced your opponent wide to the backhand, and now when you hit the ball to the forehand side your opponent will have to run farther.

Another appropriate ball would be an easy ball that your opponent hits to your forehand, allowing you to then hit the ball to their forehand side, generating a good angle cross-court. This will work especially well if you have hit four or five balls to the backhand side because your opponent will still be thinking the ball will be coming to his or her backhand and/or will be standing over on the backhand side because that is where you hit the previous balls.

When Serving in the Deuce Court

1. Serve to the backhand side 85 percent of the time (see Lesson #30 for the discussion on the Three Major Weaknesses). Serve to the forehand side 15 percent of the time. Mix them up.

2. Hit the next ball and keep hitting the balls to the backhand side until you get the appropriate ball (see explanation above), then hit the ball to the forehand side.

3. As a variation, hit another ball (two in a row) to the ·forehand side.

4. Then go back to step 2.

When Serving in the Ad Court

1. Serve to the backhand side 85 percent of the time. Serve to the forehand side 15 percent of the time. Mix them up.

2. Hit the next ball to your opponent's forehand side.

3. Hit the next ball and keep hitting the balls to the backhand side until you get the appropriate ball, then hit the ball to the forehand side.

4. As a variation, hit another ball (two in a row) to the forehand side.

5. Then go back to step 3.

As you may have gathered, the idea of this strategy is to maximize hitting to your opponent's weaknesses. You have hit the ball to your opponent's weaker side and made your opponent hit running forehands and running backhands. And if you hit any of your balls deep, you have made your opponent hit balls that are that much more difficult for them. By hitting two balls in a row to your opponent's forehand as a variation, you may be able to "wrong foot" them, therefore keeping them off balance.

When Returning Serve

If The Ball Is Served To Your Forehand

1. Hit all forehand return of serves to the forehand (left) side (see Lesson #32 for my reasoning for returning the serve cross-court).

2. Hit the next ball and keep hitting the balls to the backhand side until you get the appropriate ball, then hit the ball to the forehand side.

3. As a variation, hit another ball (two in a row) to the forehand side.

4. Then go back to step 2.

If The Ball Is Served To Your Backhand

1. Hit all backhand return of serves to the backhand (right) side (see Lesson #32 for my reasoning for returning the serve cross-court).

2. Hit the next ball to the forehand side. As a variation, hit another ball (two in a row) to the forehand side.

3. Hit the next ball and keep hitting the balls to the backhand side until you get the appropriate ball, then hit the ball to the forehand side.

4. Then go back to step 3.

Notice that when a ball is served to your forehand, the strategies are the same in both the deuce and ad court.

Notice that when a ball is served to your backhand, the strategies are the same in both the deuce and ad court.

One last thought about this strategy -- you still must be able to execute it. If you are having difficulty, start with just hitting all of your balls to your opponent's weak side and work on being consistent. Consistency is the first and last strategy to use against your opponent (see Lesson #29).

Lesson #39 - A Basic Doubles Strategy

Most, if not all, of the following doubles strategy I learned from Dick Leach, who was the coach at USC for a number of years. When I was in college, doubles was my best game (my partner and I were undefeated), and I thought I knew a lot about how to play it. After I started teaching, Dick invited me up to his tennis camp in Big Bear, California, to play and enjoy some time off. It was here that I observed what Dick was teaching about doubles strategy. I was amazed at how little I really knew. What he taught made so much sense, and I, of course, stole his ideas and began to teach my students the same strategy.

Dick has put together a more complete booklet of his doubles strategy and he has made it available to me. If you purchased this book from my web site you received this doubles booklet as a bonus. For those others of you who want to get this booklet, it is available on my web site for a nominal fee.

When You Are At the Net

Always hit your volley at the opposite net person (this includes the overhead). This shot is most effective when aimed at knee level of your opponent. If you, by chance, actually hit your opponent, just say you are sorry, but do not change your strategy.

When and how to change this strategy: If your opponent has great reactions and is returning most of your shots, then hit your volley three feet to the outside part (toward the doubles line) of that person.

Where To Stand And What To Do When You Are At Net And Your Partner Is Serving

Stand in the exact center of the service box, and when the ball hits the court, move in a straight line directly toward the center strap, stopping when you get three feet from the net. Remember to hit the ball at the opposite net person if you are able to hit the ball. If you cannot or do not hit the ball, you must back up, all the way to the "T" if possible.

When and how to change this strategy

When you have lost two points on the deuce side from having your opponent hit a return of serve down the line, you must change your strategy for that side. Likewise, when you have lost two points in the ad court, this also means you must change your strategy. Notice that these changes in strategy are independent of each other. So, when one of these situations occurs, you will move straight in, or if the serve is hit wide, you will move in at an angle parallel to it. If your opponent returns most balls high over the net or hits a lot of lobs, then you must adjust and maybe not move forward at all.

Where To Stand And What To Do When You Are At Net And Your Partner Is Receiving The Serve

Stand on the service line in the middle. When your partner returns the ball and *IT GOES PAST THE NET PERSON,* then you will move in toward the center strap. Again, remember to hit your volley at the net person. If you cannot or do not hit the next ball, you must back up to the T, if possible. If you are playing at a high level, then these movements are shortened because the speed of the ball going back and forth will not give you much time to move very far. This does not mean that you don't make an effort to move some.

When and how to change this strategy

When you have lost two points on the deuce side from having your opponent hit a ball down the line, you must change your strategy. Likewise, when you have lost two points in the ad court, this also means you must change your strategy. Now you will move in toward the net, following a path parallel to the ball. If your opponent lobs this ball a lot, then you cannot move in toward the net and be ready to move back so you can hit the lob.

Where To Stand And What To Do When You Are Serving

When Serving In The Deuce Court

When you are serving in the *deuce court*, it is *absolutely critical* that you serve the ball most of the time *to your opponent's backhand* (assuming that he or she is right-handed). Most of the time means 90 percent of first serves and 100 percent of second serves. So, how far you stand from the center line depends on how well you are able to serve to the backhand. If you are having trouble serving to the backhand when standing over from the middle, you must move to the center line to assure that your serve goes down the middle to the backhand. If by chance you are standing in the middle and you serve to the forehand, you must then move over to the right to protect an angled return of serve wide to your forehand.

When Serving In The Ad Court

When you are serving in the *ad court*, you must also serve the ball to the *backhand side most of the time*. Although it is not as critical as in the deuce court, the percentages stay the same. You should stand over about eight to 10 feet from the center line so that it is easier to serve to the backhand.

For help on serving more accurately, see Lessons #21 and #44.

Where To Stand And What To Do When You Are Receiving The Serve

When Receiving In The Deuce Court

If you are receiving in the deuce court, you want to stand far enough to the left so that you can hit as many forehands as possible (assuming that your forehand is your best shot), but not so far over that the server can hurt you with a wide serve. Most of the time you will want to return the serve cross-court and back to the server.

One of the dirty little secrets of doubles is that most of the time the team that returns the most balls wins the match. In order to do this you must figure out a way to return the serve into the court no matter what.

For more on the return of serve, see Lesson #14.

When Receiving In The Ad Court

If you are receiving in the ad court, again, stand far enough to the left so that you can use your forehand (assuming that it is your best shot) but not so far that you get into trouble if the ball is hit down the middle.

The Basic Rule On Where To Be Positioned When At Net

When your partner is hitting the ball and he or she is at the baseline, then you should be back on the service line so you can play defensive should the ball be hit to you.

If your opponent is at the baseline and he or she is hitting the ball, then you should be moving in toward the net so you can play offensive should the ball be hit to you. However, you should not be moving in until the ball has *passed the net person*.

As the title says, these are just basic strategy rules. Doubles is a very complex game, and there are many variations to the above strategy such as poaching, signaling, playing Australian doubles, serving and going to the net, returning serve and going to the net, hitting your return down the line, playing the angles, how to defend against poachers, and when to lob, to name more than a few. However, when you master this basic strategy, your value as a doubles partner will be measurably enhanced.

Chapter 4 - Strokes and General Information

Lesson #40 – The Mother of All Stroke Tips - Holding the Follow-through

Well, maybe not the Mother, but certainly one of the children. I do believe, however, that this is one of the "miracle" tips for improving your strokes as well as your consistency in hitting the ball into the court, but it will take some focus and concentration.

Here is what you are to do: hold your follow-through until you see your ball bounce on the other side of the net. This means that your arm will come to an absolute stop. Do this even if you miss the ball. In fact, it is even more critical to hold it longer when you miss.

When you are holding, pay attention to the location of your follow-through and how relaxed you are. This is the time you will relax your grip and arm, maybe to the extreme. You are not trying to follow through correctly or to make anything happen.

You will also hold and relax your footwork. As a bonus while doing this exercise, work on seeing the ball to your racket some of the time, and some of the time work on your breathing. If you can do all three in the same period of time, that would be ideal.

This exercise has a lot of benefits. The foremost is that it will absolutely *groove your stroke.* It will make you *more consistent* in hitting the balls in the court. It will force you to learn how to be *balanced with your footwork. And best of all, it will help you break the pattern of reacting physically to your shot.*

Speaking of reacting physically to your shot, do you know when you do this and what it looks like? Here are some questions to ask yourself to see if you ever react to a shot.

- Do you ever make a verbal sound when you miss? Some of my student make a sound but are not aware of it until I point it out to them.

- Do you look away immediately when you miss or even if you hit a great shot?

- Do you look down at the ground (hang your head) after a shot is missed?

- Do you pump your arm when you hit a winner?

- Are you aware of any other physical pattern that you do when you either miss a shot or hit a winner?

Here are some other things to watch out for when doing this exercise. You will have a tendency to not hold the stroke when you miss and not even know it, so you must be very aware and allow yourself to hold even longer at these times. In addition, you will have a tendency to not allow the stroke to come to an absolute stop every time, so you need to be especially aware of this. Remember that this is not the time to worry about hitting the ball into the court. It is much more important to hold your follow-through, even if it means that you miss the next ball because you are not ready for it.

You will also need to be aware of whether you fall off balance when you are holding your footwork. If you find that you are off balance, it means that your legs are too tense, so you will have to relax them until your body can figure out how to keep your balance.

The short version of this exercise is to just allow your arm and your footwork to come to a complete stop before you recover to the ready position. However, if you have difficulty with this, then you will need to go back to holding until your ball bounces on the other side.

Lesson #41 - How to Give Yourself a Lesson Every Time You Play

Once you really learn this technique, you can apply it to every physical skill that you may ever want to learn. Of course, here I will address using it to learn tennis strokes.

1. You first must know exactly how to hit the stroke you want to practice. *This is your goal or ideal stroke.* You must know it so well that you can teach a beginner. If you don't know exactly how you want to hit your stroke, you can still use this technique, but you will bypass step 2 and start with step 3.

2. Take some practice swings without the ball, starting from the ready position and making certain you are able to *do these practice swings absolutely perfectly every time.* Take as many of these swings as needed until you can stroke it relaxed and without thinking too hard about how to do it. In order to make sure that you are taking the practice stroke correctly, you may need to follow your stroke with your eyes as the racket goes through your entire swing and especially into the backswing.

3. Before you start hitting the ball, decide what part of the stroke you want to work on. Choose only one part at a time, and plan on spending a few minutes on each part. *I would start with the follow-through because I believe this is the most important part of the stroke.* Then I would spend a few minutes on the grip and the wrist to make sure that they are relaxed. Next I would go to the backswing, followed by the path of the racket as it goes forward to the contact with the ball, and then the footwork.

4. So, starting with the follow-through, you will just *be relaxed, feel the arm and observe the racket moving to wherever they both finish up.* This needs to be done with as little effort as possible. When you make your stroke as relaxed as you can, your body will learn very quickly how to follow through correctly, and later on when you are not thinking about the stroke, your body will still stroke it the way you were practicing it.

5. As you compare your stroke with "the ideal stroke" and you are aware that your stroke is not going where you want it to, then stop hitting the ball and take a number of practice swings without the ball using an absolutely perfect swing. It would also be helpful to visualize this perfect swing and/or talk to yourself about the swing. Then go back to step 4 and just be relaxed and feel your stroke again.

6. If your stroke is not getting close to your practice swing or is not improving, it means you are trying too hard to control your stroke, and you will need to relax some part of your body more. Another issue some people have is that they are trying so hard to just hit the ball that they don't do a very good job of *feeling the stroke.*

7. While you are following the instructions listed above, do not be concerned about where your ball is going or try to hit the ball into the court. Your awareness is to be on

your stroke (body awareness) and not on the ball. As you get better at feeling your stroke, it would be helpful to add seeing the ball or being aware of your breathing. Do not try to do both at the same time. If you find yourself missing too many shots, you could fix this by visualizing your ball going into the court and then letting go of any thought about this and just getting back to *being relaxed and feeling your stroke again.*

8. **Lastly, you are not to use this technique in a match. This is only for practice and/or warm-up.**

Lesson #42 - Ground Strokes: A Checklist of Things to Practice

This checklist is just a guideline for you. It includes some issues that I feel are important to take a look at from time to time. As you practice, you should be adding some of your own personal stroke issues to this list. When you practice, you can use the process in Lesson #41 to work on your own issues as well.

- Hit all balls harder that are above the net and not too deep.
- Hit more top spin on low balls and down-the-line balls.
- Make sure to do a complete follow-through, especially on backhands and high backhands.
- Exhale through the mouth in a relaxed way, with a sigh just before and through hitting the ball.
- When returning serve, gently exhale with a sigh just as your opponent hits the ball and continue exhaling through your hit.
- Take a split step just as your opponent hits the ball.
- If you are missing the return of serve, hit the ball a little easier, using a more relaxed stroke.

- If you are having trouble returning serve, hold your follow-through until it comes to a complete stop.

- If the stroke is not feeling proper and if you feel the need, take a practice swing without the ball.

- Allow the racket to rotate over the ball as contact with the ball is made.

Lesson #43 - Serves: A Checklist of Things To Practice

As with Lesson #42, this checklist is a guideline on some issues that I feel are important to take a look at from time to time. As you practice, you should be adding some of your own personal stroke issues to this list. When you practice, you can use the process in Lesson #41 to work on any of these issues.

- See the ball spinning as it is tossed into the air, and see the blur of the racket as it hits the ball.

- See the ball as it goes over the net and to the opponent's racket.

- Bend your knees a little when serving. Rotate shoulders on the serve.

- Always hit a slight amount of side spin on the first serve.

- Exhale through the mouth in a relaxed way, using a sigh, just before hitting the ball.

- If you miss a serve, take time to visualize the ball going into the court before your next serve.

Lesson #44 - Serves: Questions to Ask If I Am Missing My Serve

Below are some questions you may want to ask yourself if you are missing your first serve a lot. I believe that you should be hitting 75 to 80 percent (or higher) of your first serves in. If you are not, then by asking yourself these questions and actively adjusting what you are doing, you will see your first-serve consistency improve.

The same applies for your second serve. If you serve more than one double fault a set, then you need to take a look at what is going on and make some adjustments.

- Am I seeing the ball to the blur of the racket?
- Am I following the ball as it goes over the net?
- Have I visualized the serve, including seeing the ball, the speed, the stroke, and the exact path of the ball (two to six inches over the net) immediately before I serve?
- Am I taking enough time before I serve to truly do a complete and thorough visualization?
- Am I gently exhaling just before I hit the ball and keeping the exhale long through the hit?
- Am I relaxing my grip and/or my wrist enough as I make contact with the ball?
- Am I relaxing my arm enough as it goes through the swing?

Lesson #45 - Volleys: A Checklist of Things To Practice

This checklist is a guideline for you. It includes some issues that I feel are important to take a look at from time to time. As you practice, you should be adding some of your own personal stroke issues to this list. When you practice, you can use the process in Lesson #41 to work on any of these issues.

- See the trajectory as the ball comes to your racket.
- Hit any volley that is above the net hard.
- Take a split step at the moment your opponent hits the ball.
- When hitting volleys, *be sure to always keep the handle lower than the head of your racket.*
- Exhale through the mouth in a relaxed way, using a sigh just before and long after hitting the ball.
- Have your racket continue 12 to 18 inches after hitting the ball. This means that you want to hit through the ball as if it isn't there.

Lesson #46 - Read Ron Waite's Articles

Ron Waite is a certified USPTA tennis instructor who took up the game of tennis at the age of 39. Frustrated with conventional tennis methods of instruction and the confusing data available on how to learn the game, Ron has sought to sift fact from fiction.

In his seven years of tennis, Ron has received USTA sectional ranking four years, has successfully coached several NCAA Division III men's and women's tennis teams to post season competition, and has competed in USTA National singles tournaments. Ron has trained at a number of tennis academies and with many of the game's leading instructors.

In addition to his full-time work as a professor at Albertus Magnus College, Ron photographs ATP tour events for a variety of organizations and publications. The name of his column, TurboTennis, stems from his methods to decrease the amount of time it takes to learn and master the game of tennis.

Ron has some terrific articles on just about all aspects of tennis. If you are really serious about your mental game, as well as learning about a wide variety of subjects, go on my Web site, www.maxtennis.com, and you can find the links to all his articles in "Tennis Articles – Outlined" and/or the full articles located in "Tennis Articles on the Mental Game." I have not read any articles by anyone that are better.

Chapter 5 – Tennis Drills

The following drills will help you develop your physical game, but more importantly will help you discover what state of focus and relaxation your body needs to be in for you to play at the top of your game. If you find that you are not playing at a higher level and becoming tougher mentally, then you are not playing the mental game correctly. And, most likely, you are trying too hard and therefore are too tight in some part of your body. So, just do the opposite of what you have been taught in the past: *Try less, relax some part of your body more, let go of judging your shots, and stop thinking about winning. Really work on getting your conscious mind out of the way and letting your other than conscious mind direct your body. In other words, revisit the Core Principles.*

Practice your ground strokes as explained below in Drills #1, #2, and #3, and then go back to Drill #1 and start again using the volley. I find that if you place small orange road cones on the court as targets, this will help you be aware of where your ball is actually landing in relation to your ideal. I will address the serve in later drills. *Any time you practice, don't just hit down the middle.* Spend 95% of your time hitting forehands cross-court, backhands cross-court, forehands down the line, and backhands down the line. After a while, play a game up to seven points while still hitting cross-courts and down-the-lines. I will expand on those drills later.

I have also included here all the drills and ways to practice that I told you about in some of my other lessons. I repeat them here so that you can not only find them more easily but also so you will be reminded again to do them. All of these drills are very important to the development of both your physical and mental game.

The way I see someone getting the most out of these drills is to *take this book with you* when practicing and refer to it often. The important part of each drill is what I call "*mind awareness.*" The *questions to ask yourself* are the key to improving the *mind awareness.*

Drill #1: Seeing The Ball

Spend five minutes or any period of time you want just *seeing the ball* (Lesson #2). Seeing the ball means *focusing* on the ball and being able to tell yourself at all times what direction the ball is spinning. Seeing the ball means *consciously* seeing what direction the ball is spinning as the ball comes over the net, after the ball bounces, all the way to the blur of your racket, and all the way to your opponent's racket. It also means *consciously* seeing the ball spinning when you miss the shot long, wide, or into the net.

In order to see the ball completely, keep thoughts about your stroke or hitting the ball into the court out of your head. Just focus on the ball spinning. In addition, make seeing the ball easy. Relax your eyes. Just think about when you read. You don't try hard to see the words, you just do.

Questions to ask yourself after a point or rally is over:

- Am I seeing the ball spinning all the way to my racket?
- Am I seeing the blur of the racket as the ball hits the strings, or am I seeing the ball to the presence of the racket?
- Am I seeing the ball spinning after the bounce?
- Am I seeing the ball spinning after it leaves my racket, all the way to the net and to the other side of the court?

- Am I seeing the ball spinning, even when I hit the ball long, wide, or into the net?

Any "no" answer means that you have some more practicing and letting go to do.

- Am I worrying about hitting the ball into the court?
- Am I trying to hit the ball into the court?
- Am I worrying about stroking the ball correctly?
- Am I trying to stroke the ball correctly?
- Am I trying to direct the ball to a certain spot on the court?

Any "yes" answer means that you have some more practicing and letting go to do.

Drill #2: Paying Attention to Your Breathing

Spend five minutes or any period of time you want *paying attention to your breathing* (Lesson #3). Paying attention to your breathing means *consciously feeling yourself exhale.* The ideal breathing pattern is to allow your breathing to be *very relaxed,* to use a long exhale with a sigh before you make contact with the ball and to *continue exhaling through the hit.* Paying attention to your breathing means *consciously* feeling your breathing, even after the point or rally is over. The idea is to be able to do this over an extended period of time.

To do this exercise properly, you will have to keep thoughts about your stroke or about hitting the ball into the court out of your head. Focus only on your breathing. You also need to know that you may or may not hit the ball very well, and you need to let go of this. This exercise is not designed to maximize hitting the ball into the court. It is an exercise of relaxing and letting go.

Questions to ask yourself after a point or rally is over:

- Am I *consciously* feeling myself exhaling?
- Is my breathing very relaxed?
- Am I sighing before the hit and continuing it after?
- Am I *consciously* and continuously aware of my breathing even between points and into the next point?
- Am I able to stay focused on my breathing, even when I hit the ball long, wide, or into the net?

Any "no" answer means that you have some more practicing and letting go to do.

- Am I worrying about hitting the ball into the court?
- Am I worrying about stroking the ball correctly?
- Am I trying to direct the ball to a certain spot on the court?

A "yes" answer to either means that you have some more practicing and letting go to do.

Drill #3: Combining Seeing the Ball and Breathing

Spend five minutes or any period of time you want *working on consciously seeing the ball and consciously feeling your breathing at the same time.* Again, you must keep your mind free of thoughts about hitting the ball into the court or about your stroke. Focus only on the ball spinning and your breathing. Refer to the questions to ask yourself in Drills #1 and #2.

Drill #4: Feeling Your Strokes

The most important part of the stroke is the follow-through. Spend five minutes holding the follow-through until it comes to a complete stop. This means stopping and holding the footwork also. *When you combine holding the follow-through with consciously seeing the ball spinning or consciously feeling your breathing, this becomes an extremely powerful exercise* (see Lesson #40).

Spend five minutes on each stroke doing the following: *without controlling or judging,* consciously feel your complete forehand from the time you are in the ready position to the time you recover back to the ready position. Then spend five minutes with the backhand, five minutes with the forehand volley, and five minutes with the backhand volley or any other stroke you want.

While you are *consciously* feeling the stroke, keep thoughts about hitting the ball in the court out of your head. When you get comfortable with feeling your stroke, add either seeing the ball spinning or your breathing, but not both.

Questions to ask yourself after a point or rally is over:

- Am I *consciously* feeling the direction the arm and racket travels on the backswing?

- Am I *consciously* feeling the direction the arm and racket travels as the racket starts forward?

- Am I *consciously* feeling the direction the arm and racket travels as the racket goes forward and makes contact with the ball?

- Am I *consciously* feeling the path of the arm and racket after the racket makes contact with the ball?

- Am I sure that I know exactly where my follow-through ends? *(Remember that the follow-through is the most important part of the swing.)*

Any "no" answer means that you have some more practicing and letting go to do.

Drill #5: Maximizing the Balls Going into the Court

After you are comfortable focusing on the ball and feeling your breathing, you are ready to work on maximizing the number of balls going into the court. Refer to the Mental Game Core Principles in Chapter 1.

Using the drills explained above and spending as much time as needed on each drill, do the following:

For a period of time, work on *consciously* seeing the ball spinning (as in Drill #1) primarily, then secondarily but at the same time *consciously* feel yourself breathing (as in Drill #2). For another period of time, work on your breathing primarily, then secondarily but at the same time focus on seeing the ball. *Every time you miss the ball*, take the time to visualize or talk to yourself about exactly where you wanted the ball to go. *If your stroke doesn't feel right, relax it more the next time.* If after revisualizing and/or talking to yourself the ball doesn't go more consistently, then you are too tight somewhere in your body and you must relax more. Start with relaxing your grip and/or your wrist.

As you get comfortable with these drills, add the playing of points (up to seven) and see how (if at all) your focus and concentration are affected. *If your shots change once you start the game of seven, then you know that you have some more letting go to do.*

If you have trouble focusing when you start playing points, ask yourself these questions:

- Am I trying to win? If yes, you must know by now that trying doesn't work. Only seeing the ball, breathing, and relaxing properly does. If you play better than your opponent does, winning will take care of itself (Lesson #1). *Your job is to find what state of mind you need to be in to maximize your learning and your play.*

- Am I trying to stroke the ball correctly? Am I thinking about my stroke? If you answer yes, you will need to let go and trust that your body will do this for you.

- Am I making *consciously* seeing the ball and *consciously feeling* my breathing the most important thing in my life when I am playing? Even if you make it important, you don't need to try hard to do it.

Drill #6: A Running Drill

Do Drill #5, but this time you will *hit your balls to alternate sides* while your practice partner will hit to one side only. When the person running gets tired, switch. The purpose of this drill is twofold. The one hitting from side to side gets to practice seeing the ball and breathing while hitting a change-of-direction ball. The runner gets to practice seeing the ball and feeling his or her breathing while running and hitting.

Some variations if you have problems with your focus:

- Spend some time just *consciously* watching the ball and forget about your breathing.
- Spend some time just *consciously* feeling your breathing and forget about the ball.
- Combine seeing the ball and breathing.
- Pretend that someone will pay you $1 million for every time you can see the ball and breathe properly. That is just about how important you must make your focus.

Questions to ask yourself:

- On the balls that I have to run hard for, am I still able to see the ball spinning to my racket, and am I still able to feel my breathing and taking a long exhale just before and through hitting the ball? If your answer is no, you need to let go more.
- When I am aiming my ball, am I trying so hard to aim that I have not watched the ball and been aware of my breathing first? If your answer is yes, you need to learn to let go more and let your body do the aiming while you are busy seeing and breathing.

Drill #7: Another Running Drill

Do Drill #6, but this time one of you will *hit your balls anywhere* while the other will hit to one side only. When the person running gets tired, switch. The purpose of this drill is twofold. The one hitting from side to side gets to practice seeing the ball and breathing and deciding where to hit the ball for maximum effect. The runner gets to practice seeing the ball and feeling his or her breathing while running.

The real value of this drill is to find out what state of mind you must be in to choose where you want the ball to go. You do it by making sure that the thought of where you want the ball to go is just a knowing, and it must follow in third place behind seeing the ball and being aware of your exhaling. And when you know where you want the ball to go, let your other than conscious mind direct your body.

Questions to ask yourself:

- When I miss the ball, am I really seeing the ball and feeling my breathing first, or am I putting aiming the ball first?
- Am I trying too hard to hit the ball to where I want it to go? If your answer is yes, you need to relax more, starting with your grip and wrist when you make contact with the ball.
- On the balls that I have to run hard for, am I still seeing the ball spinning to my racket, and am I still feeling my breathing and exhaling just before hitting the ball?

Drill #8: Volleys

You can use all of the above drills to practice volleys as well, keeping the following ideas in mind.

In my opinion, breathing properly is the most important thing to do while volleying. If you are serving and volleying, see if you can feel your breathing as you are moving to the net. If you are just standing at the net, practice feeling your breathing first (using a relaxed exhale before and continuing after you hit the ball) and at the same time, but secondarily, work on seeing the ball.

Drill #9: The Return of Serve Drill

Here is the best way to practice your return of serve. You must have a willing opponent, which means that you can only do it in practice matches and not in tournaments. You can even do it in doubles if all four of you agree to practice it (see Lesson #14).

- The point cannot start until the return of serve has been returned into the court.

- If you missed the return on your backhand side, your opponent must then serve all serves to your backhand until you get it back into the court. If you missed the return on the first serve, then your opponent will serve another first serve. If that first serve is missed, then your opponent will serve a second serve, but it still must be to the backhand side until you get it back. If your opponent misses the second serve, he or she will keep serving until the ball is in play. This means that he or she cannot double fault. This way you get to practice until you get it right.

- If your opponent serves an ace, then the challenge for him or her is to hit another ace. If you miss the return on the first serve, then the challenge for the server is to hit two first serves in a row. If the server double faults, he or she will have a chance to practice a second serve. That way the server gets to practice also.

This drill will allow you to do the return of serve over and over without worrying about losing the point. It also takes the advantage away from the server, as the server doesn't get a free point just because he or she hit a good serve. It is a terrific way to work on one of the most important shots in tennis.

Drill #10: The Lob and Overhead Drill

Here is an easy way to practice both the lob and overhead if you have a willing partner who will do this drill with you when you are playing a practice match (see Lessons #33 & 34).

Hit the first ball to make your opponent hit a volley, then hit a lob on the return of that shot. When you hit your lob, do not try to just feed it to him or her. Go for the perfect lob cross-court. If your opponent hits an overhead back to you, hit your opponent another volley (not a lob), and then hit another lob if he or she returns your shot. Your opponent should be hitting overheads for winners. This way you both can warm up practicing what you would do in an actual match. *See lesson, #34, about why you want to hit your overhead as hard as you can.*

Here is my reasoning: using this drill, you can practice your lob every time you warm up, assuming you are playing with someone you know who wants to warm up this way. By only hitting a lob from a volley, you will be practicing hitting a lob like you would in a match. When you hit your lob, make sure your breathing is relaxed, and you see the ball spinning all the way to the blur of your racket. Since I consider the lob to be a "touch shot," relaxing more as you hit the ball is a must.

Drill #11: The Bounce/Hit Game

Every time the ball hits your racket or your opponent's racket, say out loud or to yourself "hit." Every time the ball bounces on the ground, say out loud or to yourself "bounce." Check to see if you are saying "hit" with a relaxed voice or a tense one. And check to make sure that you are saying these words exactly when it is happening and not before or after. Spend any amount of time doing this. Even try it in a practice match, but if you do, say the bounce and hit to yourself and not out loud.

Drill #12: The Spinning Game

Another game to play is to say out loud or to yourself what direction the ball is spinning. When you hit the ball, say what direction it is spinning as it is going over the net and again when the ball is coming back toward you. Don't forget to consciously see the spin after the bounce.

Drill #13: The Trajectory Game

Here is another game to play. Watch the trajectory of the ball as it comes to you and as it goes back to the other side. Ask yourself whether the ball is still rising, has reached its peak, or is dropping when you hit it. Do the same when your opponent is hitting the ball.

Drill #14: The Listening Game

If you have done the bounce-hit exercise that I explained in Drill #11, then this concept of listening is very similar except that you are hearing the ball instead of saying "bounce" or "hit". Of course, you will want to see the ball at the same time.

Just hear the ball bounce on the ground and hear the sound that the ball makes when it makes contact with the racket. Hear these sounds on both sides of the court. Try this in a practice game situation and see what happens.

Chapter 6 – Two Fun Quizzes

A Little Quiz

Take this quiz (if you are feeling a little smart).

1. What is the most important part of the stroke?
2. How do you know if you are executing the stroke properly?
3. What is a good way to practice the forehand and backhand?
4. What should you do when you start the rally but you are not playing a match?
5. If you find you are not stroking a particular stroke properly, how can you fix it?
6. When you are practicing your strokes, what should you refrain from doing?
7. If you want the ball to go into the court, what should you refrain from doing?
8. If you want the ball to go into the court, what should you be doing?
9. When you miss a ball, how can you practice hitting it into the court using a perfect stroke without actually hitting more balls?
10. When you are serving, where should your front foot be placed?
11. When you are serving, how can you practice your toss?
12. Where do you want to aim most of your serves and why?
13. What is the most important strategy to use when you are playing a match, if you want to win?

14. How do you win?

15. Where do you want to aim most of your shots and why?

16. What is important to know about your grip, wrist, and arm?

17. How can you find out if your grip, wrist, or arm is too tight?

18. How do you make sure you are using the correct grip?

19. Are you checking once in a while to make sure that the "trigger finger" is spread out away from the other fingers? How do you do this?

20. What is a good way to warm up your serve and practice your swing at the same time?

21. Where do you want your balls to go when hitting forehands and backhands?

22. How do you maximize your performance?

23. How can you practice your tennis when you are off the court or cannot play?

Answers to the Little Quiz

1. What is the most important part of the stroke? <u>The follow-through.</u>

2. How do you know if you are executing the stroke properly? <u>With body awareness. Feel your arm stroking the ball.</u>

3. What is a good way to practice the forehand and backhand? <u>Hold your follow-through until you see the ball bounce. If the follow-through is not correct, then relax and fix it before you recover.</u>

4. What should you do when you start the rally but you are not playing a match? <u>Take a perfect stroke every time you start the ball. Make sure to start some rallies with a backhand.</u>

5. If you find you are not stroking a particular stroke properly, how can you fix it? <u>Take a practice stroke without the ball. Visualize a perfect stroke. Hold the follow-through and fix it before you recover.</u>

6. When you are practicing your strokes, what should you refrain from doing? <u>You should refrain from thinking about where the ball is going.</u>

7. If you want the ball to go into the court, what should you refrain from doing? <u>You should refrain from thinking about your strokes.</u>

8. If you want the ball to go into the court, what should you be doing? <u>You should be watching the ball, breathing, and relaxing.</u>

9. When you miss a ball, how can you practice hitting it into the court using a perfect stroke without actually hitting more balls? <u>Visualize or talk to yourself about exactly how you would like the ball to go, with a perfect stroke.</u>

10. On the serve, where should your front foot be placed?

119

Two to six inches behind the baseline.

11. When you are serving, how can you practice your toss? By tossing the ball into the air, keeping your arm up in the air, and seeing if the ball falls into your hand.

12. Where do you want to aim most of your serves and why? To the backhand, because that is usually your opponent's weaker side.

13. What is the most important strategy to use when you are playing a match, if you want to win? Keeping the ball in play by hitting it easy, aiming three to six feet over the net and right down the middle.

14. How do you win? If you maximize your performance, and play better than your opponent, winning will take care of itself. Maximizing your performance is a better goal than worrying about beating your opponent.

15. Where do you want to aim most of your shots and why? If you are a beginner, you should hit the ball three to six feet over the net, right down the middle. As you get better, hit your balls to the backhand of your opponent.

16. What is important to know about your grip, wrist, and arm? That they must be relaxed.

17. How can you find out if your grip, wrist, or arm is too tight? By paying attention to or feeling your grip, wrist, or arm as you hit the ball.

18. How do you make sure you are using the correct grip? By paying attention to, or feeling, all five fingers on the racket.

19. Are you checking once in a while to make sure that the trigger finger is spread out away from the other fingers? How do you do this? By paying attention to your trigger finger as you hit the ball.

20. What is a good way to warm up your serve and practice

your swing at the same time? <u>Take a series of continuous swings, making sure you are loose, allowing the arm to bend completely behind your back, and making sure that your follow-through is on the left side (if you are right-handed).</u>

21. Where do you want your balls to go when hitting forehands and backhands? <u>If you are a beginner, you should hit the ball three to six feet over the net, right down the middle. As you get better, hit your balls to the backhand of your opponent.</u>

22. How do you maximize your performance? <u>See My Mental Game Core Principles.</u>

23. How can you practice your tennis when you are off the court or cannot play? <u>By practicing mentally using visualization, talking to yourself, or fantasizing about playing perfect tennis. Use the Beach CD (See the end of this book).</u>

A Big Quiz

Take this big quiz (if you are feeling really smart).

Once you think you are ready, here is a quiz to check if you are really able to see the ball.

1. What direction is the ball spinning after the bounce?
2. What are the patterns of the spin (how your ball spins most of the time) on your forehand?
3. What are the patterns of the spin (how your ball spins most of the time) on your backhand?
4. Can you tell yourself on any given ball whether it is spinning fast, slow, or medium?
5. Have you ever seen the ball traveling through the air when it had no spin?
6. Have you ever really seen the ball spinning after the bounce on the return of serve? Is it any different from the answer to question #1?
7. Have you ever spent a great deal of time seeing the ball and breathing every second for more than one point?

Answers to the Big Quiz

1. What direction is the ball spinning after the bounce? The ball always has top spin on it after the bounce. The only exception is when someone serves a ball fairly hard with side spin. Then the ball will begin to have top spin but will still be spinning sideways. Don't take my word for it. See the ball for yourself.

2. What are the patterns of the spin (how your ball spins most of the time) on your backhand? There is no way that I can answer this question. However, do you ever see side spin or under spin, or do you just assume you know what kind of spin you are putting on the ball? The key to this answer is that you must see for yourself.

3. What are the patterns of the spin (how your ball spins most of the time) on your backhand? See #2 for this answer, as it is the same.

4. Can you tell yourself on any given ball whether it is spinning fast, slow, or medium? Again, the key to this answer is whether you ever notice the difference in how fast the ball is spinning and with enough awareness to tell someone else about what you have observed.

5. Have you ever seen the ball traveling through the air when it had no spin? The thing about a ball that has no spin is that it should stand out like a sore thumb because it is so rare. If you can't answer yes to this question, then you need to become more aware of the ball.

6. Have you ever really seen the ball spinning after the bounce on the return of serve? Is it any different from the answer to questions #1? See the answer to #1.

7. Have you ever spent a great deal of time seeing the ball and breathing every second for more than one point? If you ever can do this, it is the way to getting into a trance state that will allow you to truly play out of your mind.

Improve Your Mental Focus with this Special Audio CD

After completing my book, I found that in my own tennis game I couldn't focus the way I wanted to. Of course, I knew what I wanted to focus on, but I just felt I needed some help. I decided to try a hypnosis program designed for the mental game. After listening to it, not only did I think that it was not very useful, but I thought that I could put together a more effective hypnosis CD myself. That was when I went to see Dave Dobson to ask for his help in making this happen. I have known Dave Dobson for over 20 years (see below for his background), seen him privately, and taken his Fun Shop on communication a few times.

Not only did Dave come up with a terrific idea on what we could do for a hypnosis CD, but he has contributed greatly to helping me modify my wording in this book so that it speaks to the other than conscious mind more efficiently.

Since Dave already had a self-hypnosis CD, he figured we could customize it easily and use it for improving one's tennis game. This CD has already been proven effective by years of usage by many different people, so there is no doubt that it would prove helpful for anyone who wants to go the extra mile and really improve his or her mental game through the other than conscious mind.

The "Beach" CD by Dave Dobson

With the CD, you will also get complete information on how to use it for your tennis game. It is very easy to do, and you will find it very effective. Since you have purchased my book, if you are interested in purchasing this CD, I have arranged a

15% discount for you off the regular price. Just go to this page on my web site (www.maxtennis.com/products.htm), where you will find the special promo code. So when you click on the link there, it will take you directly to Dave's order page, and by putting in this code, you will get the discount.

About David R. Dobson, Ph.D.

Dave comes from a background that includes business and a private practice of clinical hypnotherapy and psychotherapy that spans more than 45 years in Los Angeles and the U.S. West Coast.

In business he has been owner and manager of a highly successful executive search firm and division manager and director of sales for an international plastics company with a sales force of more than 200 people.

These experiences and his need to find models of communication that work led him to develop concepts he calls "Other Than Conscious Communication," an outgrowth of his model of psychology that he calls "No Fault Psychology."

Since his move to the San Juan Islands off the Washington coast in 1977, he has traveled well over a million miles conducting seminars and trainings throughout North America and Europe. His psychological models and concepts, which transcend traditional communication, have become highly respected tools for personal growth both in mental health fields and the corporate community.

Go to his Web site, www.otcc.com, to get more information on what he does.

Index

P

play in the zone, 14, 16, 17, 33, 123

playing your best, about, 41, 71

points, playing (see Lessons #18, #19, & #20), 35, 49, 62, 65, 73, 83, 90, 91, 105, 111

points, what to do between (see Lesson #15), 23, 35, 56-58, 108

practicing, about (see Chapter 5 - Drills) 18, 41, 46, 52, 55, 62, 73, 114

practice and breathing, 35

practice and warming up, 62

practice lob (see Lesson #33), 81-83, 115

practice running and hitting, 73

practice seeing the ball, 62, 111-113

practice swing, take a, 57

practice the mental game (see Core Principles), 13, 14, 25

practice the wondering technique, 75

practice volleys, 113

practice your strokes (See all Lessons in Chapter 4), 95, 102

practice your weaknesses, 71, 72

Q

questions to ask yourself, 27, 41, 43-46, 55, 56, 58, 59, 65, 69, 101, 106-113

R

Ranney, David (resume), 15

return of serve (see Lesson #14 & #32), 52-56, 88, 90, 92, 99, 100, 114, 122, 123

return of serve and breathing (see Lesson #14 & #32), 34

return of serve, articles on, 92, 102

return of serve, how to practice (see Lesson #14 & #32), 54, 55, 114

running and hitting (see Lessons #25 & 30), 72, 73, 78

running and hitting with breathing (see Lessons #25 & 30), 73, 111

S

secrets, 29, 37, 92

seeing the ball (see Lesson #2), 26-31

seeing the ball, secret page on, 29

serving (see Lessons #21, #22, #36, #43, #44), 34, 61, 62, 86-91, 100, 101, 114, 117, 119

serving strategies, 87, 91, 92

singles strategy (see Lesson #38), 86-89, 117, 119

strokes (see Lesson #40 & 42), 14, 16, 21, 23, 27, 30, 43, 49, 61, 63, 95-100, 117, 119

Stuart, Ken, Owner of Palisades Tennis Club, 5, 11, 28, 29

T

tie-breakers (see Lesson #19), 60, 64, 65

turn your game around (see Lessons #8, #9, #11), 18, 42

W

Waite, Ron (see Lesson #46), 56, 102, 103

warming up (see Lesson #17), 52, 60-63, 64, 79, 82, 99, 115, 118, 120

weaknesses (see Lessons #24 & #30), 41, 59, 71, 72, 78, 79, 87

winners, hitting (see Lesson #23), 59, 71, 82, 115

winning (see Lesson #1), 19, 25, 41, 59, 60, 64-66, 71, 105, 111, 118, 120

wondering technique (see Lesson #27), 24, 75